Endpapers *(left to right)* Sir Simon of Wensley, *circa* 1375, Wensley, Yorkshire; William Wardyworth, 1533, Betchworth, Surrey; Robert Lond, 1461, St Peter's, Bristol; John Young, titular Bishop of Callipolis, *circa* 1525, New College, Oxford.

Father John Y. Simm

A CONNOISSEUR MONOGRAPH
General Editor: Frank Davis

Anglican Church Plate

James Gilchrist

THE CONNOISSEUR
and MICHAEL JOSEPH
London 1967

Designed and produced for The Connoisseur,
Chestergate House, Vauxhall Bridge Road, London SW1,
and Michael Joseph Ltd, 26 Bloomsbury Street, London WC1
by George Rainbird Ltd, 2 Hyde Park Place, London W2
Filmset in Linofilm by Graphic Film Limited, Dublin, Ireland
and printed and bound by Kultura, Budapest, Hungary.
House Editor: Mary Anne Norbury
Typographer: Nan Quelle

First published 1967

Contents

Acknowledgements

The publishers and producers wish to express their gratitude to the museums, collectors and photographers who have courteously assisted the author in obtaining the material for the illustrations reproduced in this book. They would especially like to thank the following:

The Bishop of Birmingham, The Bishop of London, The Bishop of Ripon; The Dean and Chapter of Bristol Cathedral, The Dean and Chapter of Coventry Cathedral, The Dean and Chapter of Lincoln Cathedral, The Dean and Chapter of Westminster Abbey, The Dean and Chapter of York Minster. The Rectors and Churchwardens of Basingstoke, Hampshire; Birdham, Chichester; Caversham Heights, Berkshire; Hill Ridward, Staffordshire; Kirkby Mallory, Leicestershire; Nettlecombe, Taunton, Somerset; St Augustine's with St Faith, London; St Dunstan's Church, Stepney, London; St James Church, Piccadilly, London; St Mary with Christ Church, Wanstead, Essex; St Michael-le-Belfry, York; St Michael's Church, Basingstoke, Hampshire; St Nicholas Church, West Itchenor, Sussex; St Peter Mancroft, Norwich, Norfolk; St Peter Port, Guernsey; Staunton Harold, Leicestershire; Trewhiddle, Cornwall; Vowchurch, Herefordshire; Wolverton, Warwickshire. The Vicars and Churchwardens of Sutton Weaver, Cheshire; Brampton Abbots, Herefordshire; Charsfield, Suffolk; Chediston, Suffolk; Dunmow, Essex; Cirencester, Gloucestershire; Cumnor, Berkshire; Dagenham, Essex; Dunham-on-Trent, Nottinghamshire; Digby, Lincolnshire; Ellenhall, Staffordshire; Hornchurch, Essex; Norbury, Staffordshire; Norwell, Nottinghamshire; St Andrew's Church, Bradfield, Berkshire; St Bartholomew's Church, Brighton, Sussex; St Mary-in-Coslany, Norwich, Norfolk; St Pancras Church, London; Staunton, Shropshire; Weeke, Hampshire; Willingham, Lincolnshire; Wetheringset, Suffolk; Wickham Market, Suffolk; Wool, Dorset. The Rt Hon. Lord Balfour of Burleigh; The City Museum and Art Gallery, Birmingham; Corpus Christi College, Oxford; John Freeman Ltd, London; The Glasgow Art Gallery and Museum (The Burrell Collection); The Hinckley Times, Hinckley, Leicestershire; Brand Inglis, London; Ipswich Museum, Suffolk; A. F. Kersting, London; Komminister Evert Andreasson, Bokenäs, Sweden; The Ministry of Public Buildings and Works, London; The National Trust, London; New College, Oxford; Gerald Pates, Gloucester; The Royal Scottish Museum, Edinburgh; St John's College, Oxford; Derrick Witty, London; The Worshipful Company of Goldsmiths, London

6

List of Colour Plates

List of Illustrations

9

1 Introduction

There are more visitors to English cathedrals and parish churches than ever before. Such observers soon become aware of intimate connection between the evolution of the ecclesiastical buildings and its possessions, and the lay and political history of the nation. The epitaphs on tombs tell of battles in every corner of the globe, of civil reforms and of gentle uneventful lives, such as are lived by many of the sightseers themselves. The carvings in stone and wood illustrate the fashions in dress and manners. The hour-glass on the pulpit tells of the custom of long sermons, which provided Thomas Fox with the excuse that he fell asleep and, when he was suddenly woken up, used "a participle" in the sermon time. Box pews point to the growth of class consciousness from the days of Elizabeth I.

There is, also, increased interest in church restoration, a source of controversy between those who would have nothing changed or restored and those who claim that the building, with its furnishings, to have any meaning, must live, and that the *raison d'être* for the building and its furnishings is to be the setting for the showing forth of the Word of God in sacrament and sermon. The first Celtic and Roman missionaries to the Anglo-Saxons would erect a cross and an altar, a covering that has been gradually elaborated to the honour of both Word and Sacrament until we arrive at our present-day cathedrals and churches.

The Cross and candlesticks on altars suggest the mysteries of the building's basic purpose, but the vessels for the Celebration are out of sight except when in use.

Because the Eucharist is the central act of worship of a living body, the devotions and the doctrinal emphases which surround it are constantly changing within the limits which the teaching of the church allows. The ceremonial simplicity of the house church of the first Christian centuries flowed naturally over the years into the splendour of the high Middle Ages. This splendour in the Reformed Church of England,

reverted again to a startling simplicity, which in places became careless-
ness towards the Mystery of the Eucharist, then gradually elaborated
into the magnificence of the High Church of the nineteenth and
twentieth centuries, whilst today, 1966, there is a return to a studied
simplicity. Thus it is that the story of Anglican church plate depends as
much on theology and sacramental devotion for its forms as on artistic
taste. The artist and craftsman have but a limited scope, for they are to
make vessels within limits set by the theologian, and their personal
artistic feelings must be largely subordinated to precise details. It must
be remembered that each object used in and for the services and rites
of the Church is functional and significant. Where this is not so, the
rites become cluttered with archaic detail and slowly lose their significance. Until the Reformation, the Church of England was an integral —
if strongly independent in many matters — part of the religious life of
Western Europe. Its church plate was similar to that of the rest of the
Catholic Church, although the characteristic national avoidance of
artistic extremes prevented our artists from following the florid and
flamboyant gothic fashions of the Continent, if we can judge from the
pitifully small amount of church plate that has survived the royal confis-
cations of Henry VIII, the regents of Edward VI and the change in the
shape of the vessels insisted upon by the reformers. So it is that the
history of Anglican church plate falls into two distinct periods, pre- and
post-Reformation. Both of those periods can be sub-divided as the
shape of the communion vessels changed with the shift in emphasis in
Eucharistic thought and as new forms of devotion developed.

It is difficult for present generations to understand that the first
Christians were neither interested in nor sentimental about the vessels
that the Saviour used at the Last Supper. The reality of meeting Him
sacramentally, the showing forth of the Risen Lord and the fellowship
of the common meal were the purpose of their meeting. At the Last
Supper Jesus, we are told, took the Cup. There were several cups used
in the Jewish Paschal meal. It seems probable that the cups would be no
different from those in everyday use at that period. An ordinary family
would use earthenware or glass, while a wealthy family might use
silver cups. The type would no doubt be the two-handled vase-shaped
cups that were then in common use. It was not until Christianity ceased
to be proscribed and became the state religion of the Roman Empire
under Constantine the Great (274–337), that pilgrims began to visit
the Holy Lands. It was then that the places connected with Jesus' life
became important through their association with Him, and gradually
relics became of interest. In the eighth century the Venerable Bede
described the Cup of the Last Supper; a cup of silver which held rather
more than a pint. The cup was vase-shaped with two handles. There is,
indeed, a cup in Valencia Cathedral which it is claimed is that used at the
Institution of the Communion, although the evidence of art historians
does not support such a claim. Representations of communion vessels

12

in the catacombs show vase- and beaker-shaped vessels with two handles. These paintings are some of the earliest examples of Christian art and since the chief services held in the catacombs were celebrations of the Eucharist, which took place on the anniversaries of the martyrs who were buried there, the representations of the vessels would be of those in use at that time.

Tertullian, at the beginning of the third century, mentions that glass vessels were in use for the Eucharist. In fact, glass and crystal have been used, sporadically, until present times. In the Church of Scotland there are eighteenth-century glass cups at Linlithgow, and many French cathedral treasuries possess crystal and faience cups dating from the late eighteenth century. Glass was gradually displaced by silver. However, there is a most interesting side-light into the mind of the Church as to how its possessions, hallowed by sacramental use, should be considered. When in many churches glass vessels made their reappearance during the early years of the fifth century, bishops ordered the silver vessels to be collected and sold. The money which their sale gained was used to redeem Christians from slavery or prison. Today the general rule in the Church of England is that a vessel that has been used for the Eucharist shall only be sold when it is certain that either its use will continue in another church or it will be exhibited in a museum. It is indeed a difficult question to resolve satisfactorily. Many a small church has extremely valuable plate, surplus to its requirements, and also has need of vast sums to restore its slowly decaying structure. Should the one be sold to pay for the other? Whether the pious gifts of former parishioners be alienated under any circumstances has obviously been a live question in the minds of many donors who have inscribed on their gifts of plate the hope that their gift will not be sold in future years. As far as can be ascertained faculties to sell plate for charitable purposes have not been recently applied for.

The Eucharistic Cup in the period up to the tenth century was generally two-handled, vase-shaped and made of precious metals inset with precious stones. The patens were also made of precious metals and glass.

There were, however, from the eighth century onwards official pronouncements about the material to be used for the sacred vessels. When Saint Boniface, the English missionary to Germany in the eighth century was asked if the use of wooden chalices was permissible he replied, with a comment on contemporary religion that "formerly priests of gold used chalices of wood, but now contrariwise wooden priests use chalices of gold".

Various councils during the eighth and ninth centuries forbade the use of horn, brass and copper and ordered the use of silver and gold. But even so, poor churches were allowed less expensive materials. In England the prohibition of wooden chalices was made definite by Edgar in 967, and by 1175 Richard, Archbishop of Canterbury, went so far as

13

to forbid any bishop to bless a chalice made of tin or pewter. So although, as we have seen, the early church did not hestitate to sell its precious vessels for charitable purposes, and indeed such sales were encouraged by Saint Ambrose, Saint Augustine, Saint Gregory and other holy men, in general, where donors were generous and congregations wealthy, precious metals became the rule.

By the thirteenth century Durandus (1230–1296), who made a compendium of liturgical knowledge and its mystical interpretation, had promulgated theological reasons against the use of wood and horn as well as practical ones against the use of glass and brass: "Wood since it is porous and spungy, absorbs the Blood"; "The rust which forms in brass and bronze is unseemly, while glass might break and the precious Blood be spilt." It must be recognized that the reasons he gave were derived from a growth in veneration for the Blessed Sacrament. This is a case where practical reasons for the prohibition of a custom were later overlaid with suitable doctrinal reasons.

While the two-handled vase-shaped chalices continued in use until the end of the twelfth century, they were used for the communion of the laity. The priest consecrated in a small cup, then poured a small quantity of the consecrated wine into the large two-handled cup, which was already prepared with wine. This large cup was called the Ministerial Cup and was taken by the deacons to the communicants. The Ministerial Cup was eventually withdrawn from the service and the Priest's Cup alone kept for the Eucharist. There are a small number of magnificent Ministerial Cups left on the Continent, but none in England. There is, however, one of the noblest examples of a Ministerial Cup in Ireland, which was found in Ardagh, Co. Limerick in 1868. This is thought to be of the eighth century and as Celtic missionaries played such an important part in the evangelization of England, this type of Cup would have been familiar to early members of the Church of England. Maire and Liam de Paor in their "Early Christian Ireland", 1964, write that the Ardagh Cup "could be lifted comfortably only by using two hands." It is of silver, enriched with enamel, gold, gilt-bronze and glass. The handles and two circular ornaments on the side of the bowl are decorated with enamels and gold filigree. There is a band of gold filigree with enamelled bosses round the bowl, and the foot and outer edge are set with filigree plaques and enamel bosses. Under the central band there are the names of the Twelve Apostles. This is a masterpiece, but should not be considered as exceptional.

In the early centuries of the Church each Bishop toured his diocese, visiting parishes, disciplining and admonishing errant members of his flock and seeing that the property of the churches was in good order. This duty was gradually transferred to the Archdeacons who, in addition to overseeing the clergy in matters of discipline held the particular responsibility of accounting for the property of the churches. They made, and to this day make, a visitation of churches in their Arch-

14

deaconry and "take an account in writing of all the ornaments and utensils of the churches, and also of the vestments and books, which they shall cause to be presented before them for their inspection, that they may see what has been added or what has been lost". The meaning of "utensils" is to include all the vessels of the Church which are necessary for the performance of the Liturgy. There is such a manuscript of 1368, that deals with the 350 churches under the jurisdiction of the Archdeacon of Norfolk. From this one can draw a good picture of the furnishings, books and utensils needed to perform these offices of the church. There is also a very valuable inventory of the Archdeaconry of Ely which covers the years from 1278–1390, noting the additions and losses through the years.

In 1368 the inventory of utensils for Sandringham was: "one censer, a lantern, two lamps, one silver chalice, one pewter chalice, four cruets with a bronze ewer, a processional cross painted with a crozier, a hand bell, a pyx for the Reserved Sacrament and vessels for the chrism and holy oil, all kept securely under lock and key (*sub seruris*), clapper, pewter basin, a bronze basin. Chalice given to the Altar of Blessed Mary by the Rector Alexander". The Archdeacon would compare the inventory with the list of furnishing and utensils listed in a constitution set forth by Archbishop Winchelsea (1293–1317). This had made it obligatory for the parishioners to provide a chalice, a processional cross, a cross for the dead, a censer, a lantern, a small bell for carrying before the body of Christ at the visitation of the sick, a pyx for the body of Christ, a paxbrede and a candlestick for the Paschal Candle.

We are not here concerned with the vestments or the books, although it is interesting to see that a church would need as many as fifteen books to perform the Rite, which makes clear the cry in the preface of the Book of Common Prayer of 1549, and which is still to be found at the beginning of the Prayer Book: "Moreover the number and hardness of the rules called the Pie, and the manifold changings of the Service, was the cause that to turn the Book only was so hard and intricate a matter that many times there was more business to find out what should be read than to read it when it was found out". Nowadays the service requires only the Prayer Book and the Bible: but hymn books have become by custom obligatory.

2 Pre-Reformation Plate

Chalices

The chalice is a vessel in three parts, each of which is functional and has a definite relationship to the others. The cup must hold wine and the foot must be firm so that the chalice cannot easily be overturned. They are joined by a stem with a knop (knot) which has a function determined by the Rubrics; the stem must be holdable above and below between the index and middle fingers. It is noticeable that when the faithful were given the wine there were usually handles to the chalice for ease of administration, but as gradually the chalice was withdrawn from the laity the need for a broad bowl, or two-handled bowl, was no longer important.

Towards the end of the twelfth century the practice of lifting each sacred element directly after its consecration was introduced, probably first in France. At the elevation the species were exhibited to the people, for adoration and to symbolize the offering of the Body and Blood of Christ to the Father. As it was thought by some theologians that the bread was consecrated only after the words of consecration had been said over the wine, each element was, in turn, lifted and adored. The elevation of the chalice without a knop might well be difficult: therefore the Rubric directs that there should be room for a firm grip. Thus it is that until the Reformation the proportions of chalices were ruled by the Rubric, and the goldsmith could use his art only in the decoration, proportion and quality of work. Further Rubrical directions allowed slight changes in the shape, but basically the chalice is always a cup, a stem with a knop and a base.

The Trewhiddle Chalice (Plate 1) is the earliest English chalice that remains. Charles Oman in "English Church Plate, 597–1830" dates it from the ninth century. It is five and a half inches and the bowl measures four inches in diameter. It was found some seventeen feet below the surface at Trewhiddle, near St Austell, Cornwall, in 1744; with it was

PLATE 1. The Trewhiddle Chalice;
2nd half of 9th century
height 5½ in. (13.97 cm.)
Trewhiddle, Cornwall

also found a considerable amount of money together with broken up jewellery and a silver scourge which suggests that it was loot from a pillaged monastery. The chalice is of little artistic merit for it is badly proportioned.

Although this is the only Anglo-Saxon chalice which had survived in England, it is not representative of all Anglo-Saxon religious art. It is recognized that the artistic influence of the seventh and eighth centuries Anglo-Saxons was widespread and thus one should perhaps look elsewhere for the style of Eucharistic vessels that the greater churches and monasteries would possess. The style of Anglo-Saxon work is exemplified by the Sutton Hoo treasure, so it is not surprising to find that C. H. Elburn, in the catalogue of the Charlemagne Exhibition at Aachen in 1965, suggests that the Tassilo Communion Cùp may well be of Northumbrian origin, dating from about 770. Even if it is not of Northumbrian manufacture it certainly reflects the influence of northern English artists who had travelled abroad. The Tassilo Cup is seven and four-fifth inches high and holds three pints. The bowl rests upon a ring of pearls, supported on a knop with spreading foot. The metal is copper and the whole is decorated in silver niello. On the foot of the cup are oval pictures of Theodore, Martyr; John the Baptist; our Lady and Saint Theodolinde, whilst the bowl is decorated with five oval pictures—Christ in Glory and the symbols of the four Evangelists. The spaces between the pictures are engraved with patterns and gilt; the whole is brilliant and overpowering in its beauty.

Oman has divided pre-Reformation chalices and patens into ten groups. In groups 2, 3, 4 and 5, there are twenty-one chalices; thirteen come from the graves of bishops or archbishops. It was the custom at Ordination, and Consecration of a bishop, to give to the priest or bishop the instrument of his office (*porrectio instrumentorum*), thus priests were given a chalice and bishops a pastoral staff. So when in early times they buried a priest the chalice that he had been given at his ordination was

18

put into the grave with him. Recently at the Abbey of Tyniec in Poland a gold chalice was found in a grave of an Abbot; another gold chalice was that found in the days of Elizabeth I in the tomb of Poppen, Archbishop of Treves, who died in 1047.

The chalice that was put with the priest was placed upright by the side of the body (which explains why a number are found telescoped, as the one found at Eye, Suffolk, in the coffin of one of the monks there). Oman, in his notes, quotes Geraldus Cambrensis' account of the translation of the body of Bishop William de Blois, where it is said that one hundred years after the burial: "His body was found unimpaired and the wine in the chalice with which he was buried was fresh and pure so it seemed".

Hope and Fallow, who were the pioneers of this grouping of chalices and patens, and who wrote their great monograph on chalices and patens in volume 43 of the Archaeological Journal, 1890, quote the Constitutions of William de Blois, Bishop of Worcester (dated 1230) where he wrote that among the ornaments of the church there should be two chalices, one silver for celebrations, the other pewter, not blessed, to be buried with the priest. By the time of the Reformation wax burial chalices had replaced the pewter.

In this connection it is interesting to note that when Pope Paul VI went to the Holy Land in January, 1964, he made a present of a chalice to the Patriarch Athenagoras of Constantinople. This act of His Holiness underlined the ecumenical importance of the meeting, for in making this presentation he was acknowledging that the celebration of the Eucharist of the separated Eastern churches was valid.

The endpapers of this book show brasses of priests and a bishop with their distinguishing marks, the priest holding a chalice with a Host in the bowl and dressed in eucharistic vestments, and the bishop with pastoral staff and full canonicals.

Of those silver chalices made between 1160 and the Reformation

19

PLATE 3. Dragsmark
Chalice, gilt; *circa* 1250
height 6¼ in. (17.15 cm.)
Dragsmark, Sweden

there are only seventy-seven examples left, so thorough was the despoliation of church plate that began with the plundering of the lesser monasteries by Henry VIII in 1537. If we assume that most parish churches had at least two chalices, and the larger churches and monasteries as from six to ten, as church inventories bear out, then at a conservative estimate there must have been about twenty-five to thirty thousand chalices in 1537.

There is only one chalice in Oman's Group 2, found in the grave of Archbishop Walter at Canterbury Cathedral. The broad bowl with a pronounced lip has a knop and spreading base divided into twelve lobes on a round foot.

Group 3, of which there are eleven, Oman has dated between 1180 and 1280. Eight of the group come from the graves of bishops who died between 1201 and 1307. The chalice has a broad shallow bowl with marked lip, circular stem with a knot in the centre and a gently sloping round foot. The knops are of various shapes. The illustration (Plate 2) is of the Chalice from the grave of Bishop Gravesend (died 1279) at Lincoln Cathedral.

Group 4, dated 1180–1280, are similar to Group 3, but have more elaborate knops and feet, the lobes of the knop engraved with formal foliage. It is suggested by Oman that this group are merely more expensive than Group 3, made for particular clients by first-class goldsmiths, as seen in Plate 3.

In Group 5 the bowls are now deeper and of conical shape, with

round stem, globed knops and round foot on which is a crucifix, sometimes engraved and at other times applied on the foot. From this date
it is to be noticed that all chalices have a crucifix or the sacred monogram
on the foot. This is simply an indication enabling the priest to know on
which side of the cup he communicated. (Plate 4.)

Group 6, of which there are three, date from the late fourteenth
and early fifteenth centuries. They have deep bowls and knops on stems
which match, in two examples, the hexagonal incurved feet. (Plate 5.)

The change of shape of the foot evolved from the necessity to carry
out a change ordered at the ablutions or cleansing of the vessels after
the Communion. In the fourteenth century it was ordered that the
chalice should be laid on its side on the paten to drain. Round-footed
chalices would roll when laid on their sides, and thus it was that the
foot was made hexagonal to ensure stability. The hexagonal form does
not have any significance other than practicability. Also at this time
the bowl becomes more conical so that when laid on its side the water
would drain out more easily than would have been the case with the
almost hemispherical form of the earlier chalice. These chalices were
termed mullet-footed, a term from heraldry; a mullet is a star of six
points, as is shown by the Will of Sir John Foxley quoted by the Rev.
C. R. Manning in his paper on Church Plate in 1889. Foxley, in 1378,
left to Bray a gold chalice with a round foot and to his wife Joan another
chalice "... with foot in the form of a mullet of six points and marked
in the knop about the foot with mine arms".

21

PLATE 5. Chalice, gilt; *circa* 1370
height 5½ in. (13.97 cm.)
Aston-by-Sutton, Cheshire

PLATE 6. (*Below*) Chalice and paten, gilt; maker's mark *grasshopper*, hallmark for 1479
height 6 in. (15.24 cm.)
Nettlecombe, Somerset

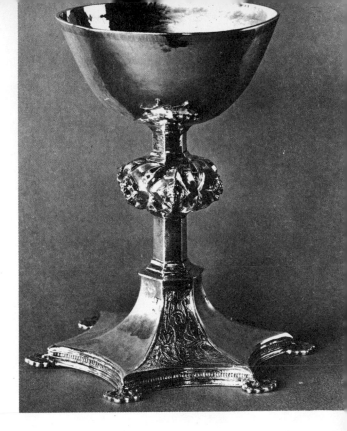

PLATE 7. Chalice, parcel-gilt;
circa 1500
height 6⅜ *in.* (16.19 cm.)
On loan to *The Victoria and
Albert Museum, London, from
Coombe Keynes, Dorset*

In Group 7, of the second half of the fifteenth century, there are thirteen chalices. The bowls become deeper and less conical, the hexagonal stems more marked with the knops variously embossed, and the spaces between the lobes sometimes pierced. The hexagonal foot is still incurved. Three of these are hall-marked, that at Nettlecombe (Plate 6) being the earliest, hall-marked 1479. On the whole the Nettlecombe chalice is the least clumsy and ill-proportioned of this group. The artists seem to have been unable to match the large knop with the base and broad shaped bowl. It may be, of course, that no work by a really first-class goldsmith has survived in this group as in Group 4.

Group 8, of which there are twenty-one, made about 1500, is similar to Group 7, except that knops are put on to the angles of the feet. It is from this time that chalices began to have inscriptions around the bowl. The Coombe Keynes chalice (Plate 7) is, without doubt, in its great simplicity, the finest of the group, although the elaborate one at Leominster is considered to be one of the finest examples of the medieval goldsmiths' art. The latter has, however, lost the knops at the angles of the foot and has the unbalanced look of Group 7.

Group 9 differs from the last two groups in the shape of the foot. It is six-lobed, not hexagonal with curved sides. There are fifteen of this group dating from 1507 to 1540. We illustrate, of this group, the gold chalice from the Chapel of Bishop Fox who bequeathed it to Corpus Christi College, Oxford. This is a superb example of English

23

PLATE 8. Bishop Foxe's Chalice, gold; maker's mark *fleur de lis*, hallmark for 1507
height 6 in. (15.24 cm.)
Corpus Christi College, Oxford

PLATE 9. (*Opposite*) Chalice, gilt; maker's mark *sceptre*, hallmark London 1527
height 7½ in. (19.05 cm.)
The Royal Scottish Museum, Edinburgh

medieval goldsmiths' art; its great simplicity of line is enhanced by the crimson and green enamel on the facets of the knop, and the lobes of the foot each side of the Crucified are decorated with figures of saints beneath canopies. (Plate 8.)

Group 10 is similar to the last save that the foot is a wavy-sided hexagon; there are three of this group, of which we illustrate the most elaborate, that from the Royal Scottish Museum, Edinburgh, hall-marked 1527. (Plate 9.)

When, by the fifteenth century, the shape of the base of the chalice was fixed, the goldsmiths were free to elaborate as much as they liked the stem, knop and calix in which the bowl was set, and so we find, on the Continent, tremendous elaboration beginning from the middle of that century. A Spanish chalice in the Victoria and Albert Museum, of the second half of the fifteenth century, has a foot divided into panels decorated with flowers and foliage, its octagonal stem has a knop formed of two tiers of open-work tracery with elaborate knops set with jewels or enamelled shields. This disciplined flamboyancy can be seen in the example from the Royal Scottish Museum.

It has been suggested that the English goldsmiths were not skilled enough to make the fantastically elaborate chalices found on the Continent; however, it must be remembered that it was always the lightest chalice that was left behind by the commissioners who were not concerned with posterity's interest in medieval art, but only in money

for the King. One cannot, therefore, expect to find any work left which would compare with that remaining on the Continent.

Patens

The paten, up to modern times, was designed to fit on the top of the chalice and was regarded as a chalice cover rather than as a separate utensil. It is seldom mentioned and when the commissioners plundered the churches they were told to leave one, two or more chalices or cups, according to the multitude of the people: but there was no word at all about patens and so it is quite plain that they were considered a part of the chalice. In medieval symbolism the chalice was frequently said to represent the tomb in which the body of Our Lord was laid, and the paten to represent the stone placed over it. When we come to the post-Reformation period the paten is almost always described as a cover, whether it be in visitation articles or injunctions. In the Arch-deacon of Canterbury's visitation, 1578, it is noted that St John's in Thanet lacks a cover of silver for their Communion Cup. The same was true of many other parishes in his Archdeaconry.

Just as it is claimed that the chalice used by Our Lord at the Last Supper has survived, so too it is claimed that the dish used by Our Lord for the bread on that occasion is in the treasury of the Church of St Lawrence in Genoa. This is a shallow glass bowl of hexagonal shape with two small handles. It has been suggested that when, in the sixth

25

century, vessels of precious metal were sold for charitable purposes the use by Our Lord of glass was ample justification for their disposal. It is much more likely, though, that at the Last Supper Our Lord used the ordinary domestic plate of His time.

There are records of large and magnificent plates, gold and silver, set with precious stones, in the treasuries of fifth, sixth and seventh-century churches. It was the custom for the congregation to bring offerings of bread which would be collected on these large plates, and one must suppose that smaller dishes or patens were used at the altar.

A paten found, with a chalice, at Riha in the Orontes Valley, Syria, in the tomb of what is believed to be a bishop, work of the sixth century and about fourteen inches diameter, is decorated with a scene of Our Lord communicating the faithful with bread and wine, and around it is a votive inscription in Greek which prays: "For the repose of Sergia, daughter of John, and for that of Theodossius, as well as for the salvation of Megalos, Nennos and their children".

It is quite clear from various writers of the second century that all members of the local church would communicate at the Sunday Eucharist, but gradually, although attendance at the liturgy was general, Communion became very infrequent. This might well be a side-light on the change of emphasis — the Communion meal wherein the commemoration of Our Lord's sacrifice was united with the grace of the sacrament slowly becoming the adoration of Our Lord present in the species and a fear of unworthy reception. Thus, by 1215, at the fourth Lateran Council, when the doctrine of trans-substantiation was officially proclaimed, it was also established that the faithful should communicate at least once a year, and this became normal medieval practice.

The breads for the people would be consecrated in a ciborium. We illustrate the Kennet Ciborium in the possession of Lord Balfour of Burleigh on loan to the Victoria and Albert Museum. (Colour Plate I.) This is English enamel of the thirteenth century. The English school of enamel work was killed by the middle of the thirteenth century by imported Limoges enamels, but there are a number of English enamels of ecclesiastical metalwork still extant, of which this is one of the finest. On the bowl are scenes of: (1) *Isaac's circumcision*; (2) *Isaac bearing logs for his sacrifice*; (3) *The angel restraining Abraham*; (4) *Samson at .Gaza*; (5) *David slaying the bear*; (6) *Elijah ascending to Heaven*. These are types of Christ's life which are shown on the cover: (1) *The Baptism of Christ*; (2) *Christ carrying His Cross*; (3) *The Crucifixion*; (4) *The Three Marys at the tomb*; (5) *The descent into Hell*; (6) *The Ascension*; all enclosed in a continuous streamer on which verses are written.

How can a thirteenth century piece belong to someone in 1092? This piece is said to have belonged to Malcolm Canwell, King of Scotland, who died in 1092, and remained in royal possession until it was given by Mary Queen of Scots to Sir James Balfour of Burleigh, from whom it has descended to its present owner.

26

The paten, therefore, on which the host was brought in (although it was consecrated on the corporal) slowly became a size convenient to be fitted on top of the chalice, and it is from this period (about 1000) that the paten was considered a cover for the chalice. The Host was a wafer of larger size than that used for the communion of the people; this was for convenience in its liturgical use, the Commixture, when a particle of the Host was put into the chalice when the words "*Haec Commixtio*" were said.

The patens now became circular with a rim and a depression which fitted onto the top of the chalice to avoid any unseemly slipping about as it was carried to the altar. Its circular central depression gradually was decorated with a various number of lobes, and the centres decorated with various paschal allusions. There is evidence from the patens of gold set with beryl and chalcedony, given to Westminster Abbey by Henry III, that they were still used separately as plates to receive the offertory, a custom which has been revived in modern liturgical movements when the faithful who intend to communicate put a wafer onto a plate on their entrance into the church.

Inscriptions on the surviving medieval chalices and patens are, for the most part, less interesting than those of the post-Reformation. The former are conventional because they are quotations from the Psalms, which refer to eucharistic devotion. Thus we find around the bowl of many chalices a quotation from Psalm 116 v.12: "I will receive the cup of salvation and call upon the name of the Lord"—this is a statement of fact for the celebrant. Another quotation reflects the desire to communicate worthily, Psalm 6 v. 1: "O Lord, rebuke me not in thine indignation, neither chasten me in thy displeasure" and one finds on a third paten Psalm 54 v. 1: "Save me, O Lord, for Thy name's sake"— again the cry of a faithful communicant.

Around the bowl of the chalice from Highworth, Wiltshire, is Luke XI, v.28: "Blessed are they that hear the word of God and keep it", and around the foot a litany suffrage: "Jesus Christ, Son of the Living God, have mercy upon us". Again, on patens, we find: "Let us bless the Father, Son and Holy Spirit".

Although by the sixteenth century quotations were sometimes blundered by the engraver, there are a number of examples of inscriptions that were made to order, as on the chalice at West Drayton, Middlesex: "Pray for the soul of John Porpyll and Johanna his wife". The inscription on a chalice left to a Sussex church in 1494 reads sweetly: "Pray for the souls of my most deirest hert and lady and mine".

The great interest of the patens, of which one hundred and forty-one have come down to the present day, is in the various subjects with which the centre has been decorated; two of the most popular were the hand of God (*manus Dei*) and the vernicle, the former being the most often used in the thirteenth century. It shows the hand of God coming out of a cloud and has reference to Psalm 144 v.7: "Send down

27

PLATE 10. Paten, parcel-gilt;
circa 1360
diameter 4⅜ in. (11.74 cm.)
On loan to The Victoria and
Albert Museum, London from
Hamstall Ridware, Staffordshire

thine hand from above". (Plate 10.) This hand of God would also be to remind those who say it that it was Christ who was being offered in the sacrifice of the Mass, for it is to be noted that in ninth, tenth and eleventh-century Crucifixion manuscript drawings the hand of God is seen frequently issuing from a cloud and pointing to the head of Christ. On the gold paten found at Tyniec the hand issuing from the clouds is shown on a plain cross. The Dragsmark paten depicts the Hand with the sun on the left and the moon on the right as they are always shown in the crucifixes of the period. This iconography brings to the mind of the priest the words of God the Father at the baptism and transfiguration of Our Lord "This is my beloved Son with whom I am well pleased, hear ye Him." (Matthew 17 v.5.)

Another popular theme was the Lamb of God, again underlining the sacrificial aspect of the offering. (Plate 11.) The sacred monogram is frequently found, and with regard to this it is interesting that at Chattisham in Suffolk the sacred monogram from the medieval paten has been inset into the foot of the Elizabethan paten cover. (Plate 12.) A large number have the vernicle—the English rendering of the true representation of Our Lord's face and features which appeared miraculously on the napkin that Saint Veronica used to wipe the face of Our Lord on his way to Calvary—as is depicted on the paten belonging to Nettlecombe, Somerset. (Plate 6.) Other themes are also illustrated,

28

PLATE 11. Paten, silver; mid-13th century
diameter 5¾ in. (14.6 cm.). Wyke, Winchester

PLATE 12. Sacred monogram on paten
Chattisham, Suffolk

such as the Trinity on the Royal Scottish Museum paten (Plate 9) and Christ in Glory on the Dolgelley paten.

We have already mentioned that as the Elevation became more general so the cross was put on the foot of the chalice. This was gradually elaborated into a crucifix, applied or engraved; others elaborated the crucifix with the Virgin and Saint John on either side. The chalice at Highworth has an interesting engraving in the place of a crucifix — Christ as a man of sorrows holding a palm branch. Christ represented as a man of sorrows is very rare in England, although common in medieval Polish and Russian art. Christ is shown wearing the crown of thorns after His scourging and mocking by the Roman soldiers. He is overcome for the moment with physical pain after the horrifying experience of a Roman scourging. One would have thought that Christ in the figure of pity would have been more usual, as the Mass of Saint Gregory was such a popular medieval picture, but we only know of one, on a chalice at Exeter of the early sixteenth century.

The paten found in Bishop Grosseteste's grave (died 1253) shows a Bishop holding his pastoral staff in his left hand and giving a blessing.

Inventories

The 1368 inventory for Sandringham (page 15) shows that the church had but the bare necessities for the liturgy; but a typical town inventory of about 1400 of St Martin's Ludgate shows five chalices and patens of weights between eighteen and twenty-four ounces, a ciborium of twenty ounces, and a cross with a crucifix of fifty-three ounces. The staff of this crucifix was of copper, with joints of silver and enamel. The censer was thirty-one ounces, the incense boat eleven and three-quarter ounces, an enamelled chrismatory eighteen and a half ounces, two reliquaries of silver and enamel of six and three-quarter and six and a quarter ounces. In other metals — copper, laten and pewter — there were two alms basins, three crosses, a ciborium, candlesticks, censers and a copper and enamel pyx, seven cruets, two small bowls, a houseling bell and another hand-bell rung in funeral processions.

The inventories of St Nicholas Church, Bristol, show a gradual increase of church plate between 1410 and 1515. In 1410 they had six chalices, two censers, an incense boat, a chrismatory, pyx and cross. The best chalice weighed fifty-two ounces, the censer thirty-three ounces, the boat and spoon twelve ounces, the chrismatory seventeen ounces, the pyx five ounces and the cross two hundred and three ounces. It may be that the chrismatory was the one bought in 1407 for 74s 11d. There is an unusual item of pewter in this inventory, a pot for god-parents to clean their fingers in after they had lifted their godchildren from the font, as the oil used at baptism would gradually leave a greasy film on the water which would cling to the hands of anyone who dipped into it.

Another interesting custom is mentioned in the notice of 1489 when they decided that they would not lend or let out of the same parish the suit of black vestments which Widow Coggan had given, although it was the custom for well-equipped churches to lend or hire out vestments to churches that were less well provided.

By 1519 the number of chalices had risen to eight, the two extra for the use of priests at particular altars.

It is interesting to note that where there are inscriptions and drawings on chalices and patens they are always mentioned in the inventory, perhaps as a means of identification. One chalice has "I will receive the cup of Salvation", three patens the Lamb of God, one a doom, another a Trinity, while the figures of the Virgin Mary and Saint John on one chalice are of green enamel.

A country village, Cratfield, in the midst of Suffolk, by the inventory dated 1528, had five chalices, parcel-gilt, two silver gilt pyxes and one parcel-gilt, a parcel-gilt censer, a parcel-gilt incense boat, two copper censers, a copper chrismatory, two large laten standing candlesticks, two small laten candlesticks and a lead gilt pax, holy water stoop and bucket.

The development of the ritual of the mass had, over the ages, necessitated many more utensils to surround the rite with dignity and magnificence. The days of one chalice and one paten as being all that was needful for the celebration of mass were far behind. With the development of the thought of the mass as having a spiritual value in itself, a value that could be put to the benefit of the quick and the dead, the growth of chantry chapels had encouraged the multiplication of altars and the furniture necessary for the celebration of mass.

Today most of us think of a chapel as a small church within a church where there can be a celebration of the Holy Communion or some other service where only a few people are expected to be present; but it was originally used to describe the furniture necessary for the celebration of mass and would include its own vessels, books and vestments and so it is we find such a great amount of plate even in the smallest village.

Before we relate how plate was disposed of, leaving each church with only one chalice and paten, we will describe the various utensils.

Pyx

From the sixth century on it was the custom to reserve some of the Blessed Sacrament to be taken to those sick and in danger of death, and it was laid down in Statutes from the eighth century on, that the parish priest must have the Eucharist ready to take it whenever called upon. The consecrated bread was kept in a small round box with a conical lid called a pyx. In different ages and parts of Christendom it was kept in various ways, but in the Church of England the pyx was ordered to be kept—like the Chismatory—safely under lock and key. The pyx would be put into an aumbry—a cupboard—usually on the north wall of the chancel—which was sometimes, in the fifteenth and sixteenth

31

centuries, elaborated into a Sacrament House. In England the pyx
was apt to be placed in a ciborium which was hung above the High
Altar; the ciborium sometimes took the form of a dove over which
was hung a cloth. The cloth from Hessett, Suffolk, now in the British
Museum, is a pyx cloth.

A quotation from Foxe's Martyrs shows that the Hanging Tabernacle
was revived during the reign of Mary: "At the coming down of the
Commissioners which was upon Thursday, 12th September, 1555, in
the Church of St Mary, and in the east end of the said Church, at the
High Altar, was erected a solemn scaffold ten feet high, with a cloth of
state very richly and sumptuously adorned, for Bishop Brooks, the
Pope's Legate, apparelled in pontificals. The seat was made that he might
sit under the Sacrament of the Altar". This was, of course, at St Mary's
Church, Oxford.

The material of the pyx seems to have been of many types. Large and
wealthy churches apparently had pyxes of crystal, beryl, gold and
silver. In 1220, when Dean William made a visitation to Mere, there were
three pyxes: one of plate for the Eucharist upon the altar; another of
silver which was used for taking the Eucharist to the sick; and a third
one of painted wood. The majority of parishes, however, in the inventories of the Archdeacon of Ely, 1287, had ivory pyxes, as were those in
the Norwich Archdeaconry inventory of 1368. In the accounts of
Dover Castle, 1344, we read: "One cup of silver gilt with its cover to
receive the Body of Christ and a cover of silk knotted to hang over the
said cup". This is elaborated in the 1361 accounts to read: "A cup of
copper gilt and a cover of silk to put over it and a pyx of ivory to be
placed inside the said Cup and to contain the Body of Our Lord". But,
for a more elaborate form of hanging pyx, St George's Chapel, Windsor,

PLATE 13. The Swinburne Pyx, gilt,
formerly enriched with enamel;
circa 1310
diameter 2¼ in. (5.71 cm.)
*The Victoria and Albert Museum,
London*

in 1385, had: "A noble ivory pyx, garnished with silver plates, gilt with a foot covered with leopards and precious stones, having a cover of silver gilt with a border of sapphires and on the top of the cover a figure of the Crucifix with Mary and John, garnished with pearls, with three chains meeting in a disc of silver gilt, with a long silver chain by which it hangs".

Henry VII, in his will, left the following instructions: "For as much as we have often and many times to our inward regret and displeasure seen at our journeys in divers and many churches of our Realm the Holy Sacrament of the Altar kept in foul, simple and dishonest pyxes, special pyxes of copper and timber; we have appointed to be made forthwith pyxes of silver gilt in great number every one to be of the value of £4, of the which pyxes we will that every house of the four orders of Friars, and likewise every parish not having a pyx of silver, gilt or unguilded, have of our gift one of the said pyxes".

The Swinburne pyx, which is of about 1310, shows the wonderful decoration that was lavished upon the pyx; one should remember that to the faithful the Sacrament reserved is the Lord Himself. (Plate 13.) The top of the cover shows the Virgin and Child; inside the cover is the Nativity. The bottom has the Agnus Dei, and inside the bottom is the head of Christ. The arcading around the side has been damaged and subjects obliterated.*

Devotion to the Blessed Sacrament was a vital part of pre-Reformation religious life and processions showing the Sacrament to the people at Corpus Christi gradually became popular throughout Western Europe. The Host was put into a monstrance; on a base similar to that of a fifteenth-century chalice there rose a fairy-like tower of pinnacles and finials, with figures of saints set in niches and in the centre a crystal glass in which was set the Host. Monstrances were not common in England but some of the larger London churches were in possession of them at the time of the Reformation.

The Reformation eliminated devotion to the Blessed Sacrament from the services of the Church and reservation, after the reign of Philip and Mary was replaced by the service of Communion of the sick. There are instances in some parishes during the eighteenth and early nineteenth centuries when the sick were communicated by the celebrant taking consecrated Bread and Wine to their house after the Communion of the faithful; the faithful would wait for the priest to return before the service was finished.

It was not until the Oxford Movement, with its increased devotion to the Blessed Sacrament, that the question of reservation was again raised in the Church of England. During the cholera epidemic at Leeds

*It has been suggested by the Editor of the English Churchman's Calender, 1952, that the reason why the Nativity and other scenes are not mutilated is because they were protected by having secular pictures pasted over them.

in 1849 the clergy of St Saviour's Church were greatly distressed that there was no Sacrament reserved for the sick; they found that there was seldom time enough for the service of Communion of the sick to be celebrated, and so at times they reserved the Sacrament and took it to the dying. Frequently one finds reservation of the Blessed Sacrament for adoration in the oratories of Anglican Sisterhoods in the second half of the nineteenth century, but it was only after the First World War that the increased demand for reservation for the sick made itself felt, and in spite of great controversy and bitterness, reservation in an aumbry, and occasionally in a hanging pyx, became more common.

The old English custom of a hanging pyx is used in Ely Cathedral, in Gloucester Cathedral and in other dioceses where faculties have been granted for a hanging pyx. One church uses the medieval canopy for the hanging tabernacle, a canopy that owes its survival to having been used as the sacristy door-stop from the Reformation to 1922.

Some fine hanging tabernacles in silver and copper gilt have been made in recent years.

Bells

When the Blessed Sacrament was taken to the sick it was usual for a hand-bell to be rung to warn people of the presence of the Sacrament, so that they could pay their reverence. These little hand-bells would also do duty for the Sanctus Bell during Mass. The bell was rung to indicate to the congregation first that the priest had reached the "Sanctus" and then again the bell was rung at the Elevation of the Host and chalice after the consecration. These bells might well be rung before the corpse in a funeral procession. The wealthy churches would have a bell for each of these purposes, but most would make one do for all. Also when the Sacrament was being taken to the sick a lighted candle in a lantern preceeded the priest. Unfortunately no bells or lanterns have come down to us, although one learns from inventories and customaries that the bells were made of silver gilt and bronze.

Cruets

These are the vessels that contain the wine and water to be used at the Communion Service.

Early in the eighth century in the Excerptions (a compilation of canons) of Egbert it states: "Let the Priests of God always diligently take care that the bread and wine and water, without which Mass cannot be celebrated, be pure and clean; for if they do otherwise they shall be punished with them who offered to Our Lord vinegar mingled with gall, unless penitence relieve them". That this is a necessary caution is shown by the instance that occurred not many years ago when a priest consecrated a chalice of red ink; the mistake was discovered by the first of the faithful few who communicated and the error was immediately rectified.

34

The wine for use at the Communion by canon must be the pure juice of the grape. In churchwardens' accounts it is usually described as wine for the Communion; but from the early nineteenth century there are frequent references to tent wine (a dark Spanish wine) replacing the claret that was cut off because of the Napoleonic Wars. The Reverend John Purchas in his "Directorium Anglicanum" (1858) notes that in the Royal chapels claret was always used, except in the German Chapel where white wine was used.

In the Archdeacon's Visitation of Norwich (1368) almost all parishes had at least two cruets, some having as many as eight. It is interesting to note that in the Ely Archdeacon's inventory, the Church of St Clements, Cambridge had four cruets in 1278, when the inventory was first made, but in the inventory made between 1365 and 1390, when two chantry chapels had been added, these also had their own cruets. There are only two pre-Reformation cruets remaining, one in a private collection and the other at St Peter Port, Guernsey. (Plate 14.) It is parcel gilt with no hall or maker's mark. It is six and a half inches in height and

35

has lost the original knop of the cover. Its globular body with long tapering neck, spreading foot, and flattened cover with thumb piece are typical of domestic vessels from the fourteenth century onwards, though this is dated about 1520. The belt which is carried round the body of the cruet is inscribed in capital letters: "SANCTE PAULE ORA PRO NOBIS" with roses for stops between the words. There is a half-length figure of Saint James the Great upside down where the handle joins the band. Engraved on the top is the capital letter "A" for Aqua. Cruets were always made and used in pairs, and so the cruet which must have had "V" for Vinum has been lost.

Cruets ceased to be used at the time of the Reformation when water was no longer added to the wine in the chalice, and in churchwardens' accounts there are references to the bottles of wine being bought for the sacrament. This wine would be poured into the flagon (q.v.), a practice followed until the Catholic Revival of the nineteenth century, when the use of water was reintroduced. The mixing of the water and wine in the chalice at the offertory was challenged by the Church Association in the case it brought in 1888 against Edward King, Bishop of Lincoln, before the Archbishop of Canterbury. The judgement ordered that the chalice should be mixed, if at all, before the service, but no notice has been taken of this judgement. In most churches today there are cruets of glass with plain and decorated silver handles. Modern artists, however, are now making them in silver to match the chalice and ciborium. (Plate 57.) It was the custom in the Middle Ages for the cruets to be of metal, silver or laten. There are numerous examples of bishops in the fourteenth and fifteenth centuries giving cruets of great value to their churches. John de Hothan, Bishop of Ely (1336) did so, the cruet for the wine being decorated with a large ruby and that for the water with a beautiful pearl. At Canterbury there were four crystal cruets. Sometimes they were decorated with representations of the marriage at Cana, while those given to be used at the Chantry Altar of the Black Prince at Canterbury were in the form of angels.

Shrines and Reliquaries
As devotion to the Communion of Saints slowly increased, and prayers of the departed saints were considered to have value, so devotion to relics of departed saints grew; as is well known there developed a business in selling relics, many of them completely bogus. To contain the relic of a saint shrines were made — large tombs covered with gilt and silver ornamentation: monasteries would indeed vie with each other for "efficient" saints to encourage visitors. The monks of Norwich, as M. D. Anderson, relates in "A Saint at Stake", invented the martyrdom of the boy William at the hands of Jews and for a short while reaped a happy monetary reward.

Smaller churches would have less elaborate copper gilt enamel boxes, about fourteen inches by six inches, to contain a relic of a patron saint. The lengths to which this decoration went can be seen from the description of the relics and jewels in the Priory of St Leonard, Norwich, which in 1422 had an ivory pyx, which held a part of the Lord's cross, and before the feet of Saint Leonard's image an ivory box contained the girdle of the Blessed Virgin and a bone of Saint Lawrence ornamented at the end with silver. On the breast of Saint Leonard were four rings placed in the form of a cross; the upper ring with a green stone, the ring on the right with a red stone, the ring on the left side with a red stone, the lower ring ornamented with a pearl and near it another ring with a green stone. Under the throat of Saint Leonard is a small brooch, on his breast a little cross, while on his fingers ten rings and five amber rosaries. In the tabernacle of Saint Leonard there was a silver image of the Count of Suffolk and a silver image of a woman and a ship of silver with anchor and chain; and on the image of the Blessed Virgin was a pectoral cross on her breast, an Agnus Dei round her neck and a sapphire ring on a middle finger.

Altar Crosses and Candlesticks
When the east ends of churches were apsidal, the altar was free-standing and approachable from all sides. The celebrant faced the congregation for the Communion Service; so we find frequent directions by canons, from the ninth to the eleventh centuries, that nothing should be placed on the altar "except a chest with relics of saints, or perhaps the four Gospels, or a pyx with the Lord's body for the viaticum of the sick". This, of course, did not mean that there was no representation of Our Lord before the eyes of the worshippers. The focal point, the conch, of the apse was very frequently the setting for a painting of Christ seated in glory; the Pantocrator Christ in Majesty, set in the mandorla of Byzantine art. For example, the centre piece of the wall paintings at Kemperley, Gloucestershire, executed about 1150, is a Christ in Majesty seated within a triple mandorla, His right hand raised in blessing, His left hand holding a book. About Him are the sun and moon, the seven golden candlesticks, the four symbols of the evangelists, the earth and stars. Although there was then no need for a cross on the altar to remind the worshippers of Christ, a forerunner of the altar cross, a cross without a staff, was carried in religious processions, as when Saint Augustine landed in Kent in 597. The staff was added to the cross for easier use when what was originally a privilege for dignitaries gradually spread to parish custom, although the practice of carrying a cross without a staff continued at the funeral procession of a child.

The processional cross was originally stationed at the side of the altar while the altar was free-standing, but in the great re-buildings of the twelfth and thirteenth centuries the apse disappeared, the rectagonal east end took its place and the altar was placed against the east wall. The paintings of the earlier period had disappeared and where there was no depiction of scenes of Our Lord's life a socket was put on the altar into

37

PLATE 15. Processional cross, copper gilt and brass; early 16th century *assembled height 73 in. (185.42 cm.). The Victoria and Albert Museum, London*

which the top of the processional cross was fixed before and after the procession. The copper gilt cross illustrated (Plate 15) shows how the whole came to pieces; this is of the early sixteenth century. Originally an altar and its surrounds were not connected with the Passion of Our Lord but rather with His glory and His triumph over death. The figure represented on the cross and in painting was the symbol of Our Lord's victory. It was not until the twelfth century that the realistic crucifix became the norm following the devotion of the preaching Friars of the Passion of Jesus.

When the cross began to be restored to the English altars in the mid-nineteenth century it was usual to have it without a figure. They were what Pugin and his followers imagined a Gothic cross resembled, with foliate ends, each having an emblem of the evangelists set with some precious stones, and almost invariably of brass. When figures were put upon the cross they were realistic in the style of the stained-glass windows of the period, copied from Continental examples.

This fitted the ethos of the Tractarians whose deep love for the Passion of Our Lord was emphasized in their devotional manuals. The Crucified Christ filled the mind with awe and love. With the change of emphasis of the Lux Mundi school, there gradually was found the victorious Christ, clothed, crowned, with arms outstretched and alive as contrasted to the dead Christ of the earlier period.

38

As artists are influenced in their depiction of the Crucified Christ by the theological temper of their time so the cross made by Louis Osman (Colour Plate II) reflects the 1960 mind of the younger theologians: Christ in his crucifixion embracing with His compassion the whole of humanity. Another contemporary example is the altar cross at Birmingham Cathedral. Silver gilt and crystal quartz, it reflects the indecision and turmoil of our present times surrounding the surety of "the Cross" at the centre of life. (Plate 16.)

During the service of the Communion there was a procession from the altar towards the people. In this Gospel procession, the Gospel book was carried and the Gospel read near the congregation; for this ceremony it was usual to have two processional candles. These candles, when not in use, would stand one on each side of the altar, although by the thirteenth century they were upon the altar, as Pope Innocent III noted: "The cross may be placed in the middle of the altar, between the candlesticks". But it must not be thought that the candlesticks and cross were yet the primary features of the altar: this was not universal until the sixteenth century. The number of candlesticks on the altar varied from place to place and service to service; from one to twenty-four were used. Squat and tripod in appearance, they were usually made of base metal, although silver candlesticks were used in wealthier churches. The most magnificent of medieval candlesticks were those used as Paschal candlesticks which held a large candle from Easter Eve until Ascension Day, the candle being lit at all services. A splendid example is the Gloucester candlestick now at the Victoria and Albert Museum. This Paschal candle represented in medieval symbolism the risen Christ seated at the north side of the chancel, the place where the Gospel was sung at Mass.

Candlesticks disappeared at the Reformation and those used by Queen Elizabeth I in the Chapel Royal caused endless discussion and grief among the reforming Fathers. During the High Church period

PLATE 16. Cross, silver gilt and crystal quartz; designed by John Donald, 1963
height 48 in. (121.92 cm.)
width 36 in. (91.44 cm.)
Birmingham Cathedral,
Warwickshire

39

PLATE 17. Candlestick, silver; maker's mark *F.L. with a bird,* 1660
height 28½ in. (72.39 cm.)
St George's Chapel, Windsor, Berkshire

PLATE 18. *(Opposite)* Cross and candlesticks, hammered silver with lapis lazuli bases; designed and made by Desmond Clen-Murphy, 1962
height of cross 33 in. (83.82 cm.)
width 26½ in. (67.31 cm.)
height of candlesticks 12½ in. (31.75 cm.)
Presented by the Worshipful Company of Goldsmiths to the Royal Air Force for the chapel at Cranwell

Laud and succeeding High Church Prelates reintroduced candlesticks on their altars. Many cathedrals have large candlesticks dating from the Restoration, but it is not until the Tractarian revival of the nineteenth century that they gradually became common, and finally today general on Anglican altars.

From the time of the Restoration many pairs of candlesticks were made for the great churches. Among the finest is the pair at St George's Chapel, Windsor (Plate 17); their baluster stems are grandly decorated with acanthus ornament and around the base are three Old Testament scenes. The whole rests upon three lions.

In recent years it has become the custom to design the cross and candlesticks *en suite* as is shown by the cross and candlesticks seen at the Royal Air Force chapel at Cranwell (Plate 18), designed and wrought by Desmond Clen-Murphy in 1962.

There is a most interesting pair of tripod candlesticks in Bristol Cathedral (Plate 19) which were given by John Romsey in 1712 and cost £114. On two of the three shields are engraved three-masted ships which are said to represent two ships, the *Duke* and the *Duchess,* of a privateering expedition in which Romsey was finanacially interested

and which returned in 1711 after capturing thirteen Spanish ships and sacking three towns.

There is one interesting reference to a mahogany three-legged candle-stick with a brass socket and taper at Bledlow in the 1783 inventory; this was used for the funeral services and might well be a reference to the custom of burying people at night.

Crucifixes
There is a tendency in some churches to multiply crosses and crucifixes. In the early church it was many centuries before Christians dared to represent the crucifixion scenes in art at all. Our Lord was represented in various forms of life and activity—as the Good Shepherd, enthroned in majesty, rising—but not dying or in death. In the Middle Ages, except for the Great Rood, isolated crucifixes around the church were rare. (Plate 20)

Chrismatory
The Church continued, from her first days, the healing ministry of Jesus. The Apostle James' exhortation to the sick states the Church's purpose

41

PLATE 19. Candlestick; maker Gabriel Sleath, hallmark for 1712
height 21¼ in. (55.24 cm.)
Bristol Cathedral, Somerset

PLATE 20. *(Below)* Pax, parcel-gilt; *circa* 1520
height 5⅜ in. (13.65 cm.)
New College, Oxford

PLATE 21. Chrismatory, gilt
brass; early 15th century
height 4¼ in. (10.47 cm.)
Ipswich Museum, Suffolk

PLATE 22. Triple oil stock
height 1¾ in. (4.45 cm.)
The Burrell Collection, The
Glasgow Art Gallery and Museum,
Glasgow

without ambiguity and also the method that should be used to treat sick Christians.

"Is any one among you sick? Let him call for the Presbyters of the Church; and let them pray over him, anointing him with oil in the name of the Lord; and the prayer of faith shall restore to health him that is ailing, and the Lord will cause him to recover." The Venerable Bede writing early in the eighth century tells us that the rite described by Saint James was still practised by the Church of England. "The sick should be anointed by the Presbyters with consecrated Oil, and that the anointing being accompanied by prayer, they should be restored to health."

The earliest forms of consecration of the oil makes it quite clear that it was to be used for every form of illness, physical and mental. Laity in the early church would anoint the sick of their own families, but by the tenth century unction began to be regarded as a sacrament, primarily for the forgiveness of sins, the supernatural curing of disease being only a secondary fruit. Gradually, unction was thought of as a viaticum for the sick man, a sacrament fortifying his soul against the terrors of death and it was this emphasis that led to its removal from Anglican church life at the Reformation.

Oil was also used from the third century in the Baptismal service, where it was regarded as signifying the Anointing of the Holy Spirit. This anointing, too, was omitted in the Anglican service of Baptism in 1549, as was the signing with the sign of the Cross with Chrism.

Every parish church previous to the Reformation had three vessels containing Holy Oils. These Oils were consecrated by the Bishop, and so it was ordered that they should be kept under lock and key. There was a difference of matter between Chrism and Oil: the Chrism was a compound of oil, made of olive oil with the addition of balm. For convenience, the oils, each in its container, were housed in a Chrismatory. The Chrismatory was a small chest, not always of precious metal. Archdeacon Swyneflete's inventory lists 337 Chrismatories in the Norwich Archdeaconry where only six were of silver or silver gilt, while about half of the city churches of London had silver ones when Edward VI's inventory was compiled.

The Chrismatory illustrated forty-one inches long dates, on the authority of Oman, to the first quarter of the fifteenth century; it is of brass, and has a roof engraved with tiling and a cresting; around it is engraved in black lettering *"Benedict DS in Donis Suis"*. (Plate 21.)

In the Burrell Collection in the Glasgow Art Gallery there is a triple

---

PLATE I. The Kennet Ciborium, enamelled copper gilt
*height 7¼ in. (18.41 cm.) diameter 6½ in. (16.51 cm.). On loan to The
Victoria and Albert Museum, London from the collection of the Rt. Hon. Lord
Balfour of Burleigh*

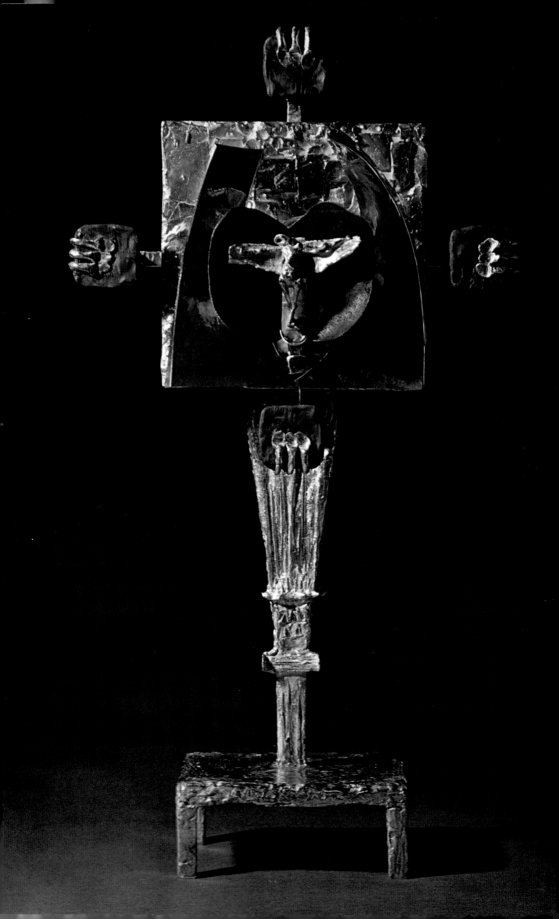

oil stock (Plate 22) which shows the letters C, S and I: these were the oils used for the sick, the catechumens (those to be confirmed) and baptism.

The most famous ampulla for oil is the one used at the Coronation of the Sovereign. It is not known when anointing was first used in connection with the Coronation service, but it is found in the Pontifical of Archbishop Egbert of York, 732–766. The present ampulla, shaped like an eagle, was renovated for the coronation of Charles II and it is said to contain some of the metal of the original. It is nine inches high and the head unscrews to admit the oil, which is poured out through the beak. Weighing ten ounces, it holds almost six ounces of fluid.

Bridal Cups

In the late pre-Reformation Sarum use there was a very pleasant custom at the end of the Nuptial Mass. A mazer of wine, in which small cakes had been soaked, was given to the bride and groom. The priest blessed the mazer in these words: "Bless O Lord this bread and this bowl, just as thou blessed the five pieces of bread in the desert and the wine at the wedding feast at Cana of Galilee. May they be healthy and sober . . ."

Cox, in his churchwardens' accounts notes that at Pilton in 1507 there was a mazer to serve brides at their wedding. There is an early Elizabethan entry referring to the silver gilt bridal cup left to St Lawrence, Reading, in 1534: "the said cup was given for the use of being carried before all brides who were wedded in St Lawrence Church, and now is termed to be occupied there at all times when need is to occupy more than one communion cup at one time".

In 1569, at St James, Bristol, there is entered payment of 2s 6d. for a little bottle to press sops in wine at any wedding and there are other references at this time to payments for bread and wine at weddings. In the stained glass at Sens there is a scene of the miracle at Cana with the governor of the feast drinking wine out of a mazer bowl.

These bowls were, of course, commonly in use as drinking bowls. Of the number that have come down to us, many have prints of religious significance and it seems possible that the mazers now still in Church possession may well have been the late medieval and Elizabethan bridal cups. In "The Taming of the Shrew" there is reference to this custom: ". . . quaff'd off the muscadel, and threw the sops all in the sexton's face; Having no other reason, but that his beard grew thin and hungerly, and seem'd to ask him sops as he was drinking." ("Taming of the Shrew" Act III s.2.)

There is another interesting reference to mazer cups in the will of

PLATE II. Altar Cross; designed by Graham Sutherland and Louis Osman, made by Louis Osman
height 48 in. (141.92 cm.). From a private collection

PLATE 23. Spoon and tray; 1789
length of spoon 9 in. (22.86 cm.), length of tray 10½ in. (26.67 cm.)
St Mary with Christ Church, Wanstead, Essex

John Beveryche who, in 1513, left to the church at Chelsfield, Kent: "A mazer cuppe for this entent that every childwife and also every bryde shall drink in it". A "childwife" was the name applied to a woman going to be churched after childbirth.

Portable Altars
Portable altars generally consisted of a small oblong slab of precious metal (such as agate, onyx or jasper) set in a frame of gold or silver which was inlaid with precious stones and enamel work. Often a relic was placed between the back of the slab and the setting. One of Saxon date, was found in a coffin supposed to be that of St Cuthbert at Durham and many earlier examples still exist on the Continent.

Licence to use and have portable altars was only given in special circumstances. Pope Innocent IV in 1251 sent a rescript to the Archbishop of York ordering, by his papal authority, and granting his beloved daughter in Christ, the Countess of Lincoln, permission to have a portable altar on which the Divine Office could be celebrated for herself and family. Henry V before the battle of Agincourt heard five masses, so presumably army chaplains were equipped with portable altars. In modern times small silver folding plates have been made for use at sick Communions.

Spoons
In medieval times spoons were needed for two purposes in the liturgy. The first spoon was used to put water into the wine, as noted previously. It was important that not more than a few drops of the water should

46

be poured into the wine, and so it became the custom to use a spoon for this purpose. So far as is known, none of these spoons have come down to us as such.

Then there were the incense spoons, used by the officiating priests to put the incense from the boat into the censer. R.L.S. Bruce-Mitford, commenting on the St Ninians Isle silver hoard, published in "Antiquity", 159, suggests that the spoon of the eight century which was found in the hoard and has a pick at one end, might have been used in the liturgy, the cutting blade of the pick to divide the Host into a definite number of pieces. After cutting, the spoon would have been used to put the pieces on to a paten.

With the Reformation there ceased to be any use for either of these spoons, but by the late seventeenth century we find spoons again being used in the Church of England. Most of them seemed to be the straining spoon from a set of teaspoons and were used to take the impurities and pieces of cork from the wine poured into the Communion Cup.

The example illustrated (Plate 23) is one that was made specially for this purpose and shows its sacred use by the form of the piercing. It belongs to Wanstead Church, Essex.

Pome

This is a ball of precious metal, five or six inches in diameter, shaped like an apple with a small hole and screw at the side. Hot water was poured into the vessel through the hole so that the priest at Mass during the cold weather, could keep his fingers warm and execute the manual actions properly. Pomes were reintroduced in churches where daily celebrations were the custom at the end of the nineteenth century.

Morse

The morse was a brooch used to fasten a cope. Frequently made of precious metal although some were richly embroidered bands with gems, it might also be enamelled. One of the favourite subjects of the medieval artist in decorating the morse (and the crook of a crozier) was the Annunciation. Such was on the morse of William of Wykeham. They were either quatrefoil or circular in shape and were three to five inches across.

At the Reformation, when copes ceased to be used the morses disappeared with them except on high feast days at Holy Communion in a very few cathedrals and at Queen Victoria's Coronation at Westminster Abbey. However, with the ritualistic revival of the nineteenth century, copes, with their morses, reappeared, and sometimes we find them made in imitation of the breast-plate of judgement that is described to be worn by Aaron in Exodus 28. More usually though they are circular plaques engraved with the sacred monogram. Recently the custom has risen of giving a bishop a cope at his consecration with the morse emblazoned with the arms of his diocese. The suffragan Bishop of

47

PLATE 24. Censer from Ramsey Abbey; mid-14th century
height 10¼ in. (27.31 cm.). The Victoria and Albert Museum, London

Lynn has a morse enamelled with the emblems representing various aspects of the life of North Norfolk — Our Lady of Walsingham, corn, shell-fish and a Pelican.

Censer
The censer, a metal bowl with a perforated cover, holds the lighted charcoal on which the incense is laid to burn. The cover is lifted off by a chain, which goes through the centre of a disc from which three chains support the metal bowl. They were usually made of precious metals and were sometimes jewelled. The covers were elaborately pierced and the Ramsey censer (Plate 24) of about 1330 is elaborately made of gothic architectural features.

The swinging censer developed about the ninth century. Previous to that incense had been burned on a brazier. This was the custom in Ely Cathedral up to the mid-nineteenth century, when, it is said, the smell of the incense disturbed the devotions of a Canon's wife, and this disturbing influence was removed.

Ritual demanded that incense be put into the censer at different times of the service and so it was offered to the priest in a boat-shaped container.

The incense boat illustrated (Plate 25) must have been specially made for Ramsey Abbey because at each end of the boat there is a ram's head.

PLATE 25. Incense boat from Ramsey Abbey, parcel-gilt; late 14th century *length 11¼ in. (28.57 cm.). The Victoria and Albert Museum, London*

49

Engraved also on the flap and on the part of the cover is a rose. The whole is a well-balanced important piece of silver.

Incense is one of the most widespread accompaniments of religious worship. It may not have been used in the early days of Christian worship because of reaction against pagan associations. It was abolished by the Reformers who, if they could have done, would have abolished bells, organs and stained glass.

When incense was reintroduced into the Anglican Church in the mid-nineteenth century, the ritualists insisted on following the old English use, copied from the far older Roman use, which involved holding the censer and swinging it, making a noise with the chains. In the old English tradition, incense was used at services other than Mass and much more simply.

People who complain about the smell of incense do so because the simple gum olibanum is not used, but a compound which contains drugs which do tend to make people feel sick or faint.

Although incense ceased to be used ceremonially from the times of Edward VI, there are frequent entries in churchwardens' accounts referring to the purchase of frankincense which make it quite clear that incense was used as a disinfectant or to perfume the building. Thus in 1588 4d. was spent at St Peter's, Winchester "for p'fume at Mrs. Palmer's buriall"; and again at Redenhall in Norfolk in 1637 6d. was spent for frankincense for the church and "sweete wood".

Cuirboulli Cases

Very frequently in the Middle Ages valuable plate was kept in cases of stamped embossed leather. At New College, Oxford there is the mitre case for the jewelled mitre of William of Wykeham. There are, throughout the country, a few cases for pre-Reformation chalices, five in Norfolk — that at Cawston is stamped with "JHESUS NAZERENUS REX JUDEORUM"—and a most interesting one at Pipe in Herefordshire. On the top of the cover of the last is "I H S", on the sides of the case two fleur-de-lis, a shield with a plain cross and a heart beneath and other shields and letters which cannot be deciphered. At Sweffling in Suffolk is a case eleven inches high and six inches in diameter and dated about 1300 which seems to have been made to carry a bottle as it has a round hole worked in the top for the neck of the bottle to pass through.

The leather case of the fourteenth century containing the "Luck of Edenhall" has on its top the sacred monogram which, it has been suggested, shows that the Luck was used at some time as a chalice. The Luck itself is a Syrian thirteenth century beaker in yellow-tinted glass with enamel decoration.

3 Introduction to the Reformation

Whilst the fifteenth century was producing beautiful works of art for the Church, there were at the same time warning voices being raised over the conduct of the clergy. Archbishop Bouchier of Canterbury appointed a Commission in 1455 to reform the clergy as the conduct of both monastic and secular clergy had become a matter of common scandal. The monks were leaving the discipline of their monastic houses for the general laxity of the secular priests and many in addition to being without proper learning, were guilty of non-residence, careless living, and "Neglecting and scorning the cures of souls to which they are bound, like vagabonds and profligates run about through the Kingdom and apply themselves to worldly gain, to revellings, moreover to drinking bouts and to wicked adulteries and fornications, and besides spend their time on all manner of vices and waste the property, goods, fruits and revenues of their benefices of this sort, and vainly and uselessly consume them on forbidden and profane objects".

Another matter that caused great discontent was the expense necessary in the making and proving of wills which were in the hands of church courts. By the early sixteenth century the scholarship, erudition and derision of scholars revealed the superstition and blatant greed and self-seeking of the ministry. Change of some kind could not long be hindered. The reforming movement which started with Luther was at first resisted on theological grounds by Henry VIII himself, but in 1529 the gradual clipping of the power of the Church began. Scales of fees were laid down for the probate of wills; fees for mortuaries were fixed, pluralities were discarded and, in general, discipline among the clergy was tightened up; the privileges of clergy began to be restricted, which, incidentally, did not cease in certain respects until 1827.

The political aspects of Henry VIII's desire for an heir and divorce from his first wife led to an act in 1534 forbidding any payment to Rome of Peter's Pence or any other Papal impositions, a declaration

51

which, in 1534, led to the King annexing for himself first fruits and tenths. In the same year the King declared England to be independent of all external authority and thus the Crown became the supreme head of the Church of England (Anglicana Ecclesia), so that it cannot be surprising that the state of the monasteries, the desire for monastic reform and the King's need for money resolved into the secularization of Church property. In 1535 Commissioners visited monasteries with fewer than thirteen inmates, accumulating information and issuing injunctions. The results of this visitation are extraordinary as seen in the introduction to the act for the dissolution of the lesser monasteries in 1536 which begins: "For as much as manifest sin, vicious, carnal and abominable living is daily used and committed amongst the little and small Abbeys, Priories and other religious houses of monks, canons and nuns where the congregation of such religious persons is under the number of twelve...", and goes on on the lines of the condemnation of Archbishop Bouchier's Commission in 1455. They suggested that the religious who were to be displaced should be sent to bigger and more serious-minded monasteries where they were to "live religiously", and they declared that: "The King's Highness shall have and enjoy his own proper use of the ornaments, jewels, goods, chattels, etc. which pertain to any of the chief Governors of the said monasteries and religious houses".

An extract from the confession of the monks of St Andrew's Priory, Northampton, though obviously the work of one of Cromwell's clerks, does show that there was also a desire to reform doctrine as well as to acquire wealth in the minds of Henry VIII and his advisers:

"We ... Francis, Prior of Your Graces Monastery of St. Andrew the Apostle, within Your Graces Town of Northampton, and the whole Convent of the same, being stirred by the grief of our conscience into great contrition for the manifold negligence, enormities and abuses of long time by us and other of our predecessors, under the pretence and shadow of perfect religion, used and committed to the grievous displeasure of Almighty God, crafty deception and subtle seduction of the pure and simple minds of the good Christian people of this your noble realm, confessing ourselves to have grievously offended God and your Highness our Sovereign Lord and Founder, as well in corrupting the conscience of your good Christian subjects with vain superstitions and other unprofitable ceremonies the very means of the abominable sin of idolatory..."

As they had not carried out the purpose for which the monastery had been founded, the monks admitted that they possessed jewels and ornaments endowed to the monastery for charitable purposes. They then acknowledged that the King had every right to take into his own possession all their goods, jewels and ornaments with other chattels, movable and unmovable, which surrender they willingly made, for they had admitted: "We, as others our predecessors called religious persons

52

within your said monastery, taking on us the habit and outward vesture of the rule St Benedict only with the intent to lead our lives in idle quietness and not in virtuous exercise, in a stately estimation and not in potent humility, have under the shadow or colour of the said rule and habit vainly, detestably and also ungodly employed, yea rather devoured the revenues issuing and coming of the said possessions in continual ingurgitations (excessive eating and drinking greedily) and farcings (stuffing) of our carrion bodies and of others the supporters of our voluptuous and carnal appetite with other vain and ungodly expense to the manifest subversion of devotion and cleanness of living and to the most notable slander of Christ's Holy Evangel, which in the form of our profession we should boast to keep most exactly, withdrawing thereby from the simple and pure minds of your Graces subjects the only truth and comfort which they ought to have by the true faith of Christ and also the divine honour and glory only due to the Glorious Majesty of God Almighty steering them with all persuasions, tricks and policy to dead images and counterfeit relics for our damnable lucre".

In considering the degeneration of the monastaries, one must remember that monastic life never recovered from the great shock of the Black Death in the fourteenth century. Houses lost large numbers of brethren; discipline, tradition and learning were weakened and no great figures appeared to reintroduce vitality to a system which had served its purpose.

It must be recognized that the dissolution of religious houses had been used in 1524 and 1528 by Wolsey, who had persuaded Pope Clement VII to allow certain religious houses to be dissolved so that Wolsey could find the money to endow his colleges at Oxford and Ipswich. Although Wolsey was, as it were, taking money for one religious purpose from another, the principle that religious houses could be dissolved became established from his precedent. Thus it is not surprising that Henry VIII, after becoming supreme head on earth of the Church of England, laid his hands on the wealth of the Church. By the time of the final suppression of the monasteries in 1538 the situation with regard to the plate of the monasteries had become slightly complicated and frequently the Commissioners would discover upon making their visitation that most of the plate had already been sold. Oman quotes the Prior of Austin Friars of Northampton who was a "great dicer" and who divided £30 worth of plate amongst his brethren; after he had been put into prison they got only £2 of it.

Through this act of spoliation some plate found itself in private hands, but for profitable rather than pious use. The nouveau riche, then, were not against this alienation of church property; while the reformers were glad to see the disappearance of the useless monasteries and the corrupt power of the ecclesiastics and Rome. Henry VIII remained a faithful adherent of the old religion to his life's end, and it was only with the succession of his son, Edward VI, in 1547, that doctrine and ritual was adapted. It is amazing that once the restraining hand of Henry VIII was removed the overpowering hatred of the old order burst forth. It was, indeed, more a revolution than a reformation that fell upon the Church of England, and in its relation to the Church of Rome it is only in these latter days that a policy of co-existence has become normal. The desire to change everything, naturally, had its influence on the furnishing and furniture of the churches.

The pillage of the monasteries in 1536 and 1539 brought about nine tons of gold and silver plate to the King's exchequer; then in the first year of Edward VI's reign the plate of the chantries and their posses- sions was confiscated for the King. This touched parish churches, which began to "loose" and sell their plate using the money they received for church expenses.

In 1548 further commissioners were sent out to make an inventory of all church goods. It was possible to obtain permission to sell plate, with the consent of parishioners, to cover the expenses of certain parochial needs; in August 1550 the inhabitants of Sandwich were given permis- sion to sell church plate to improve the harbour. But it was in 1551 that it was decreed that, since the King would need in the future a great deal of money, Commissions should be sent throughout the country to take into the King's hand such church plate as remained. So it was that the King recalled in his diary on 21st April, 1552: "It was agreed that Commissioners should go out for to take charge of the superfluous church plate to mine use and to see how it hath been embessled". The Commissioners were told that they were to leave one "cuppe or chalis" with the churchwardens "for the maintenance of dyvyne servise", the rest of the superfluous plate was to be sent to the Tower for the King's use, thus nothing would be left in church for the King to make use of in future monetary crises. The commissioners were very thorough and always left the least valuable of the chalices. For example, if there were two chalices, one gilt and one white silver, the white silver chalice would be left; if there was a parcel gilt and a whole gilt chalice, the parcel gilt would be left.

It is amazing to note the number of thefts of church plate at this time, although not all thefts were due to rapacity. Sometimes churchwardens or parishioners would hide plate and vestments hoping that better times would come in the future.

So in January 1553 Commissioners set out to steal church plate. When Mary acceded to the throne she tried to give back plate to the churches. Unfortunately, the plate had been flattened at the collecting centres and so could not be returned to use, although a number of patens were returned.

While this wholesale robbery was proceeding the services of the church were being changed. From 1548 the cup was restored to the laity. The order for Communion in both kinds was made on 1st May, and the issue of the first reformed Prayer Book was in January 1549. Although

54

Protestant churches abroad, particularly Lutherans, continued to use the ritual, vestments and sacrament vessels of pre-Reformation days, the English, in their desire for reform, were iconoclastic and the reformers in power, influenced by the Swiss, desired a wholesale change. This they finally achieved in the second Prayer Book of 1552, when all the remains of pre-Reformation custom were eliminated.

The number of Edwardian Communion Cups recorded by Oman is eighteen and their shapes show them to be designed especially to resemble a secular drinking vessel and to have as little resemblance as possible to the Massing Chalice. This shows the desire to change the whole emphasis of the service from one which was primarily an offering paid for by the laity, to a fellowship Meal in which the minister and people all had an equally important part to play. The beautiful cup and paten of St Mary, Aldermary, 1549, makers mark "W", lent to the Victoria and Albert Museum (Colour Plate III) shows well the change from pre-Reformation days. It is interesting to note on the foot of the paten cover the enamelled arms of Edward VI and around the coat of arms it has inscribed: "The body of Our Lorde Jesus Christe wiche was geven for you pserve (preserve) y (our) soule unto". These are, of course, the words directed to be used at the administration of the Body of Christ as set down in the first Prayer Book where, in full, they read: "The body of Our Lord Jesus Christ, which was given for Thee, Preserve Thy body and soul unto everlasting Life", words which were omitted in the second Prayer Book of Edward VI. This shows that, as yet, the extreme Protestant view of the sacrament was not universal and if, as Oman suggests, this cup was made for the Chapel Royal it is an interesting example of the struggle going on for the soul of the nation between the reformers and ultra-Protestants.

Oman makes a most interesting suggestion that the heavy weight, between twenty ounces and forty ounces of the Edwardian Communion Cups is due to the fact that the churchwardens, seeing that they would soon be losing their plate, used two or more chalices to turn into a Communion Cup, and as most of the Edwardian cups were made for London churches this might well show the sophistication of City churchwardens compared with their country brethren.

4 Reformation

The Reforming influence of the Lollards did not vanish from the minds of thoughtful clergy and laity after the efforts made to suppress the movement in 1401. Indeed, influence had grown through their books and preachings. Again their witness to their religion was in frequent contrast with the general run of clerics. They had been no friends to the way of thought which, too frequently in a formal way, wishes to show devotion to God in expensive gifts to church and altar. Among the conclusions which the Lollards presented to Parliament in 1384 is "That the abundance of unnecessary arts practised in our realm nourishes much sin in waste, profusion and disguise. This, experience and reason prove in some measure, because nature is sufficient for a man's necessity with few arts. The corollary is that Saint Paul says 'Having food and raiment, let us be therewith content'. It seems to us that goldsmiths and armourers (the Lollards preached pacifism) and all kinds of arts not necessary for a man, according to the Apostle, should be destroyed for an increase of virtue; because although these two said arts were exceedingly necessary in the Old Law, the New Testament abolishes them and many others."

The beauty of shrines and miraculous statues was also a snare to the Godly worship of God, for Wycliff, as early as 1380, had declared that "Pilgrimages, prayers and offerings made to blind Crosses or Roods, and to deaf images of wood or stone are pretty well akin to idolatry and far from alms. Alms to be worthy of the name were to be done to the needy man, because he was made in the image of God".

The ordinary churches were, however, not filled with treasures, but were then, as now, satisfied with the bare necessities of worship, as is shown by the illuminating inventory of the Archdeacon of Norfolk, William de Swyneflete, which, in 1368, gives a valuable picture of a part of the country that is usually thought of as wealthy with its wool trade. East Anglia was also receptive to reforms suggested by the Lollards.

Even in 1534 not all monastic houses were as well-endowed as the Romantics would have us believe. In the inventories of the suppressed monasteries of Suffolk the values were not great—for example, at Leiston Abbey the total value of the altars was 28s 8d. In the vestry were the vestments, two laten censers, two laten candlesticks, two pewter cruets, three silver chalices, two parcel gilt chalices and five silver spoons; the total value came to £3 2s 8d. This sum, together with the values of the things in the Tower Chamber, the Green Chamber, the Red Chamber, the Cloister, the Buttery, the Kitchens and the Backhouse, came to £42 16s 3d, of which the oxen, sheep, lambs and horses came to £24 3s 5d. When one sees the vast extent of the ruins of the Abbey it amazes one that the total value of everything belonging to the Abbey was only £47.

5 *Post-Reformation to 1965*

Conversion in Elizabethan Times

Queen Mary reintroduced the old worship on her accession and the cup was withdrawn from the laity.

Opportunity was also taken by some to complain of the actions of churchwardens during the reign of Edward VI. Thomas Hall, who represented the Borough of Devizes, wrote a letter to the Bishop of Salisbury, which he wished to be forwarded to the Chancellor. He complained about the misuse of the plate and jewels of St Michael's Church, Devizes by the churchwardens over a ten year period. They had sold or "otherwise consumed" a great cross worth £30, candlesticks, censers, a pyx, cruets, an incense boat and a pax to the value of £96. They had also taken bells from the belfry and they had accounted for none of this money. Thomas Hall wrote that the wardens were always promising to pay the debt, but never did. They would then call a meeting for a day when they knew that most of the parish would be away and would pass motions to reduce the debt. We have no knowledge of the outcome of this protest.

One of the first acts of Queen Elizabeth was the restoration of the cup to the laity in March 1559. Although there were certain parishes which had new cups made from the old chalice, it was not until 1561 that the bishops began to insist on the changing of the Massing Chalice into a fair and comely cup. The work of conversion proceeded from diocese to diocese as bishops gave orders in their visitation articles and injunctions; Grindle, when he was transferred to York, insisted that the Communion Cup of silver and a cover of silver be used at the Holy Communion. So it is that we find large numbers of Elizabethan cups of the same date in a particular diocese as the issue of the order.

The work was carried out by London and local silversmiths. Some cities — Norwich, for example — had a guild of silversmiths who were able to convert many of the chalices without calling on the workmen of

London, but the vast majority of work was carried out in London. The chalices generally follow the shape of a domestic beaker and have an arabesque decoration around the bowl. Some, however, have one or two raised rims that follow the line of the arabesque decoration. It might well be that this refinement, which was added by some silversmiths of the eighteenth and early nineteenth centuries, prevented the cup from slipping in the hands of the clergy and communicants as it was passed to and fro.

The finest of all the Elizabethan cups is that belonging to St-Michael Le-Belfrey, York. (Plate 26.) This was made in London in 1558 and unfortunately the maker's mark is illegible but there is no record of how it came to the church. The cover belonging to this cup has on the button a bell hanging from a cross beam, which is obviously an allusion to the name of the church. The cup has no knop and resembles in every way the wine cups in use among the wealthy.

The great interest that these cups arouse is in the variety that is found not only among London makers, but also from county to county.

One of the more prolific London makers was Robert Danby, whose work is found throughout the country, but as we can see from Plates 27 and 28 there is great difference in treatment.

When the churchwardens decided to change the chalice into a communion cup they were allowed to pay for it out of the silver of the chalice and so there was usually very little elaboration, as seen in the cup at Hornchurch, 1563, which conforms exactly to the type of a plain beaker on a capstan stem and moulded foot. (Plate 27.) The cup at Brampton Abbots in Herefordshire however, with fillet mouldings on the bowl and an elaborate stem would seem to reflect the efforts of a wealthier parish. (Plate 28.)

The work of provincial makers is somewhat uneven. The cup of St Mary-in-Coslany, Norwich has the maker's mark of an orb and cross in lozenge which belongs to a Norwich maker called William Cobbold. (Plate 29.)

Plate 30 is a cup from Wickham Market, Suffolk, with elaborate decoration and made by a local maker who used the mark of a sexfoil. It has not been discovered where this smith worked, but his marks are found on many cups in East Suffolk and he might well have been based on some small town in the Waveney Valley because another Suffolk maker, whose mark is G, converted many of the cups around Ipswich.

There is no doubt, however, about the maker of the cup shown in Plate 31, who is J. Johns of Exeter. The cup is dated 1574 and is typical of his work.

The cup at Itchenor, Sussex (Plate 32) shows another local maker and

PLATE III. St Mary-Aldermary Cup and Cover, silver gilt; London *height 7⅜ in. (18.73 cm.). On loan to the Victoria and Albert Museum, London*

many of the cups in Sussex can be ascribed to this unknown maker from their similarity in shape.

Plate 33 from Norton Lindsey shows a common Midland idiosyncrasy of the flange below the owl. Its decoration of short dashes is found throughout the country where there was no skilful engraver.

The cup at Ellenhall (Plate 34) shows another version of diamonds in place of arabesque. Some cups have a further version with a design of fish scales.

The Horsley, Derby cup (Plate 35) shows how delightful the proportions of these cups can sometimes be, as compared with the cup at Darlton, Notts (Plate 36). The trumpet stem on a spreading base of the Staunton, Shropshire (Plate 37) is a worthy piece of local manufacture, as is the cup at Thwaite, Suffolk (Plate 38), also made by the maker of the cup at Wickham Market (Plate 30). Of great interest is the paten cover. This is a saucer-shaped dish which fits over the cup and has a foot which enables it to be used as a paten. This style of paten is still wrought today. Its size, when considered with the large number of communicants then in a parish, shows that it was not originally used for bread other than wafer bread. The Royal injunctions ordered the use of wafer bread without any print on it, but some of the more Puritan-minded bishops ordered their clergy to observe a Rubric in the Prayer Book and to use such bread: "as is usually to be eaten at the table; the purest and finest wheat bread". Such was the Puritans' strength that the use of wafer bread disappeared from the early seventeenth century until the mid-nineteenth century.

The button on the foot of the paten cover is often engraved with the date of its manufacture; a number, however, are beautifully engraved with roses and other flowers. (Plate 39.) Sometimes they have the initials of the village to which they belong, showing how the name was pronounced in Elizabethan times. For example, the village of Helmingham, Suffolk is shown to have been pronounced Helmin-gam, for the initials on the button are H G.

As we have already mentioned a chalice was always expected to mean "chalice and paten", but the large number of medieval patens that remain in Norfolk allow us to surmise that many Norfolk churchwardens, when faced with the order to change the chalice into a cup, decided to save money and forget that a chalice included its paten. It is interesting to note that some medieval patens which were used for the paten-covers on Elizabethan Communion Cups have had the central design cut out, while the rest of the paten has been re-used as it was, as at St Clement's Church, Rowston, Lincolnshire, where the cover can

PLATE IV. Chalice, silver gilt; designed by William Butterfield and made by John Keith
height 9½ in. (24.12 cm.). The Victoria and Albert Museum, London

PLATE 26. Elizabethan chalice;
1558
height 9 in. (53.5 cm.)
St Michael-le-Belfrey, York

PLATE 27. Chalice; 1563
height 8¼ in. (20.95 cm.)
Hornchurch, Essex

PLATE 28. Chalice, silver, by
Robert Danby; London 1572
height 8¼ in. (20.95 cm.)
Brampton Abbots, Herefordshire

PLATE 29. Chalice; Norwich, 1556
height 6½ in. (16.51 cm.)
St Mary-in-Coslany, Norwich

63

be seen to be the medieval paten, with the IHS in the centre cut out. (Plate 40.) At Chattisham in Suffolk, however, this central decoration, in this case IHS in monogram, has been inset into the foot of the paten-cover. (Plate 11.)

In the Archdeacon's visitation in Kent, 1578, there are several references to the fact that there are no silver covers to the Communion Cup, while some have covers but are not of silver.

Stuart

The Treen-ware cup, dated about 1620, belonging to Vowchurch in Herefordshire (Plate 41) suggests that wooden chalices were sometimes used in early Stuart times. The cup is oviform on a baluster stem that rises from a circular base. The decoration is incised and consists of three birds, each within a circle, which from information given by the Rev. C. de la T. Dane, the present vicar of Vowchurch, was done by a parishioner named Hill who was a wood-turner living in Vowchurch at that time.

Other cups of this type are decorated with the Royal Arms of James I

PLATE 30. Chalice; maker's mark *sexfoil*, locally made, *circa* 1570
height 7 in. (17.7 cm.)
Wickham Market, Suffolk

PLATE 31. Chalice; by J. Johns,
Exeter 1574
height 6¾ in. (17.14 cm.)
The Glasgow Art Gallery and
Museum, Glasgow

PLATE 32. Chalice; locally made,
circa 1568
height 5 in. (12.7 cm.)
The Rector and Churchwardens of
St Nicholas' Church, West Itchenor,
Sussex

and armorial beasts. The most extraordinary feature of these vessels is the inscriptions that are to be found on them. "Drink well and welcome you that Christians be, you that have sured faith and sound repentance from every evil. Christ has made you free and from that last, most heavy, fearful sentence which driveth such into eternal fire as on the earth has every evil." "The Blood of Christ to them is drinke indeed, His word and spirit their soules but lively feede with joy and peace." "Behold what drink the Lord of Life doth give now in this life the assurance of salvation to His elect who holy do live for unto them there is no condemnation." And finally, on the foot of a mazer is written "To faithful Soules Christ giveth drinke right good; From all Sinne they are clensed by his Blood; they feel the Power of Christ's Death and Passion working in them, a true Death of all sinne and the Power of His glorious Resurrection raising UP a new lyfe to beginne of God's children it is a certain token — being Grafte in Christ shall never be broken for having faith working by sincere love; Their names are written in the Heaven above". These pious inscriptions do not necessarily mean that the cups were used for Eucharistic purposes. Indeed, neither Clifford Smith nor W. W. Watts in their articles on these Treen cups accept the opinions of H. C. Moffat in his Introduction to the "Church Plate of Herefordshire" and Cox and Hervey in

PLATE 33. Chalice, silver; locally made, *circa* 1571
height 5¼ in. (13.33 cm.)
Norton Lindsey, Warwickshire

PLATE 34. Chalice, silver; locally
made, *circa* 1580
height 6⅛ in. (15.55 cm.)
Ellenhall, Staffordshire

"English Church Furniture" that the Vowchurch cup is sacramental. There seems little doubt that the Vowchurch cup was used in the Eucharist until 1693 when the parish purchased a silver chalice. Another cup was formerly in the church at Chiddingly, Sussex. This latter parish has a silver cup of 1639 and has pricked under the lip "Bought by John Lewes for this parish of Chiddingly", which may have been especially bought because the use of the wood cup was not in accordance with Canon Law, which demanded a cup of metal. It is, however, possible to suggest that the inscriptions have a Puritan connection. If this were so, it would be a further way that the Puritans showed their independence of practice in the later years of the sixteenth century and the early years of the seventeenth. The Calvinist churches abroad used beakers at the communion and the set that belonged to the Dutch church in Norwich, (Plate 42) given to that church by "Mr. Rychard Browne of Heigham" who is thought to have been an occasional worshipper at the Dutch church, would be well known in Puritan circles. There are beakers dating from about 1600 in three neighbouring parishes in mid-Suffolk, then in the Diocese of Norwich, Hoo, Dallinghoo and Grundisburgh, a strongly Puritan district—the Royalist rector of Brandeston in their midst was burnt for witchcraft during the Commonwealth.

Sidney Jeavons in his "Church Plate of Nottinghamshire" records two beakers, one at Walesby hall marked 1598 and the other at Walkeringham hall marked 1610. These two villages are about fifteen miles apart. Ronald Marchant in "The Puritans and the Church Courts in the

PLATE 35. Chalice; locally made
circa 1580
height 5½ in. (13.97 cm.)
Horsely Parish Church, Derby

PLATE 36. Chalice; locally made
circa 1579
height 5¼ in. (13.3 cm.)
Darlton, Nottinghamshire

PLATE 37. Chalice; locally made,
circa 1600
height 4⅞ in. (12.3 cm.)
Staunton, Shropshire

PLATE 38. Elizabethan chalice
silver; maker's mark
sexfoil, locally made, *circa* 1570
height 5½ in. (13.97 cm.)
Thwaite, Suffolk

PLATE 39. Paten button showing a rose.

PLATE 40. Paten; maker's mark *Peacock and R*, possibly made in Boston, Lincolnshire, *circa* 1569
diameter 3½ in. (9.1 cm.)
Rowston, Lincolnshire

PLATE 41. Chalice, wood; *circa* 1620
height 7½ in. (19 cm.)
Vowchurch, Herefordshire

PLATE 42. Beaker, *circa* 1570–80
height 7 in. (17.7 cm.)
Castle Museum, Norwich, Norfolk

Diocese of York, 1560–1642" lists Walesby as a Puritan parish. It is, therefore, not improbable that just as the Reformers earlier in the century had eliminated any likeness in the pattern to a "massing chalice", so some extremists later had used beakers and wooden cups to make the sacrament to resemble a cottage meal, using vessels that would be in keeping.

There is, however, a beaker at Fitz, Shropshire, which is dated 1565 and which has inscribed around: "Blessed is he that comet in the name of the Lorde Osanna". The bottom of this beaker seems to be part of a medieval pyx and the sacred monogram is still visible. This inscription would show a more Catholic-minded parish priest than the later sixteenth-century clergy who ordered beakers.

Laudian Plate

We have seen that the Puritans, in order to accentuate the common meal aspect of the Holy Communion, used wine cups and beakers for the sacrament; there was naturally a reaction to this among the more

71

PLATE 43. Chalice, gilt; maker's mark *FS in monogram, circa* 1615 *height 11 in. (27.94 cm.) St John's College, Oxford*

Catholic-minded of the clergy. Laud desired to restore to the Liturgy the ritual that pre-Reformation history and tradition had employed and so while he put the altar back from the centre, longways, in the chancel to the east wall of the church, he also introduced plate that was, in shape, reminiscent of the pre-Reformation chalice.

Laud had been influenced in the arrangement of his chapel and his furnishings by Bishop Lancelot Andrewes who, for his private chapel, had placed candlesticks and an alms dish on the altar. On the credence table was a silver and gilt box for wafer bread, a small barrel set on a cradle for the wine, and a round bowl with a screw cover, out of which came three pipes. This bowl was filled with water and used to add water to the wine in the chalice. Laud had a chalice and two patens; on his chalice was engraved Christ with a sheep on his shoulder and a star on the cover.

The Laudian chalices resembled those of Oman's group 8, with knops at the corners of the hexagonal bases, well developed knops on a hexagonal stem, with hemispherical bowls, and the paten cover surmounted frequently by an orb and cross. The ciborium, with a wider bowl, was of similar shape. After the Restoration there was a further revival of these Gothic chalices among the high churchmen. (Plates 43 and 44.)

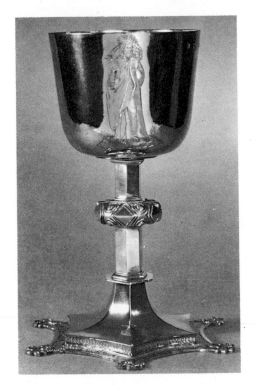

PLATE 44. Neo-Gothic chalice,
silver gilt; hallmark for 1640
height 10½ in. (26.67 cm.)
On loan to The Victoria and
Albert Museum London from
Staunton Harold. Leicestershire

What is most interesting is that when Laud, as Bishop of London, gave a Communion Cup at Manningtree in 1633 he gave a beaker-shaped cup, set on a trumpet stem, with a moulded foot and with his coat of arms engraved on the bowl. (Plate 45.)

This high church revival of Andrewes and Laud in the seventeenth century produced over seventy chalices, all of great beauty. It made little impression though, on the general run of new plate which continued to be more akin to secular cups of the time, as at Chickney, Essex, where the cup of 1617 is typical of the wine cups of the period. (Plate 46.) There is one design of stem and foot which suits the beaker even more than the Elizabethan stem, i.e., the trumpet foot, as we see in the cup from St Augustine's Church, St Faith-under-St Paul's, London (Plate 47) and at Norbury (Plate 48).

The Laudian practice was to use a covered standing paten as a ciborium. (Plate 49.) These gradually became a plate on a small trumpet foot.

In the eighteenth century the Communion Cups follow variations of the beaker shape on a stem with round base. This is shown by the cup illustrated (Plate 50), by Paul de Lamerie. Very few eighteenth-century cups are of such fine workmanship; the paten is rimmed to fit the top of the cup exactly, the stem with the knop towards the bottom, was designed

PLATE 45. Chalice of Charles I, silver; bearing the arms of Archbishop Laud, 1633 (*Below*) the inscription on the bottom of the base
height 7½ in. (19.05 cm.)
Manningtree, Essex

to facilitate handling. The weight of the cup by Paul de Lamerie at Chediston, Suffolk, ten and a quarter inches high, is twenty-two ounces; while a cup of the same design made by Elizabeth Godfrey in 1763, eleven and three quarters inches high, only weighs nineteen ounces. These long-stemmed cups with the deep bowl are extremely difficult to use where the communicants kneel at the altar rail, and while there is evidence that there were eighteenth-century churches where the communicants sat and had the Elements brought to them, there is no evidence that this was the case with these large cups. That at Kirkby Mallory, similar in shape to a Counter-Reformation Continental chalice, was eleven and three quarter inches high and would also be difficult to use.

From the middle of the eighteenth century on, Communion Cups took on the shape again of everyday drinking vessels, some with egg-shaped bowl, simple stem and knop. The influence of the Adams brothers is plain in the Communion set from St Bartholomew's Church, Birmingham (Plate 51), so it is safe to say that the eighteenth-century shape of

PLATE 46. Chalice of James I;
circa 1617
height 5 in. (12.70 cm.)
Chickney, Essex

the sacramental vessels was largely determined by tradition or taste, with no ecclesiastical influence. In the early days of the nineteenth century this continued to be the rule and for a short time a large number of cups similar to that at Cumnor (Plate 52) were given to churches. This, indeed, was a shape that was most unsuitable for use in church, for if the cup was tipped when little wine remained it was difficult to regulate the flow. Also such chalices were awkward to clean.

Gothic Revival

The freedom from ecclesiastical demands which had allowed the silversmiths to follow secular tastes was challenged by the firm opinions, strongly expressed, of the Cambridge Camden Society. The Tractarian movement was centred at Oxford around the persons of Keble, Newman and Pusey. It aimed at defending the Church of England, which they wished to re-emphasize was the Catholic Church in England and so of Divine institution. This was shown by the Apostolical succession of her Orders and by the pure and primitive form of her services as found in the Book of Common Prayer. The movement is regarded to have been started by Keble's sermon on 14th July, 1835; he preached on "National Apostasy", led to this subject by the plan to suppress ten Irish Bishoprics. The leaders interest in primitive and medieval Christianity was for purely intellectual and theological reasons. They accepted without question

PLATE 47. Chalice of Charles II, gilt; maker's mark, *IG* within a heart
height 9⅞ in. (25 cm.)
St Augustine with St Faith's (formerly at St Faith-under-St Paul's), London

the rubrics of the Book of Common Prayer and were not excited to add any ceremonial to the services of the Church. But the Romantic movement had inspired interest in the art and customs of the Middle Ages. The Cambridge Camden Society, founded by J. M. Neale in 1839, allied the artistic with the theological and directed the liturgical and ceremonial revival in the Church of England. Soon the Society had a commanding influence on the High Church party and was most definite in its views on the arrangement and furnishing of churches, views which are only now being challenged with success, so mesmerized did the clergy and laity become by the ecclesiologists.

They produced a magazine which spread their ideas and pilloried unmercifully any architect or clergyman who did not follow the school of Early English architecture. They raised the dignity and decency of public services and though nowadays it is fashionable to belittle their work, they did succeed in preventing the ruin of many buildings. It was not, however, until 1842 that their attention was brought to bear on church plate, when in the October number of "The Ecclesiologist" the following letter was printed from a young architect, William Butterfield, who was a Tractarian in churchmanship and had come under the influence of the Camden Society.

"Sir,—I wish your Society would engage some goldsmith in the

77

PLATE 49. Covered paten, silver gilt; maker's mark *hound sejant,* dated 1653
height 8½ in. (21.59 cm.)
Fulham Palace, London

PLATE 50. (*Opposite*) Beaker-shaped chalice and paten; by Paul de Lamerie, 1724
height 10¼ in. (26.03 cm.)
Chediston, Suffolk

manufacture of chalices of the ancient form, and also make it known how unfit for even the reverent performance of the Communion office are the present long deep cups in general use, on account of the difficulty of draining them thoroughly. The chalice at Corpus Christi College, given by Bishop Fox, the Founder, is exceedingly beautiful, and would be an admirable model; and also that in the possession of Trinity College, from St Alban's Abbey, both figured in "Shaw's Ancient Furniture". Goldsmiths must be checked for they are running perfectly wild in their designs for what they call 'Gothic Church plate'." ...

The Editor noted:

"The proper shape of a chalice is a somewhat shallow circular bowl on a stem *provided with a large knop for the convenience of holding,* with a base generally octangular. Many of our readers will have observed that this is the form (we believe) invariably found when chalices are represented upon brasses. We have had occasion in private applications to recommend the old form in many quarters, and we gladly take this opportunity of extending our suggestions. We know not

whether our funds will ever allow us to follow out our correspondent's hint about supplying goldsmiths with suitable designs: it is a subject however deserving careful consideration."

There was justice in the warning against "Gothic church plate" given by Butterfield. The popularizer of the "Gothic" in metalwork was A. Welby Pugin, who had published, in 1836, "Designs for Gold and Silversmiths". These designs were for secular and ecclesiastical vessels, and in style were tortuous, involved, over-elaborate and romanticized Gothic. Pugin (1812–1852) was the son of a French émigré draughtsman who worked for Nash. His interest in Gothic architecture grew after a visit to France; the flamboyant style threw him into raptures and, incidentally, led him to the Roman Church which he joined in 1834. His importance lies in his continual proclamations that Gothic was the only possible Christian style; that a good building or article for Christian use could only be in the Gothic style and in addition, could be built or made only by a Christian Catholic architect. The struggle that the Camden Society waged was not against Gothic or against Pugin's theory that the moral value of the artist determined the artistic value of

the artist's worth, but against the foreign Gothic; they claimed that for the English Gothic revival only the Early English style was appropriate. This contention must be set against the background of a warfare, which continues to this day, between those liturgical reformers in the Anglican Church who look to the Continental Roman Church for their inspiration and those who prefer to adapt the Medieval English customs of the Sarum use to the silences of the Book of Common Prayer. As the desire for a more elaborate ritual grew from the 1840's on, the need for a book directing and advising the clergy was filled by manuals of ceremonial: the ceremonial described was founded on the current Roman directories and the Gothicism of Pugin. The suggestions of Butterfield were frequently disregarded for elaborations designed by Hallam. The cry of "No Popery" that was raised against the Tractarians and their followers had the unfortunate result of fixing the position — artistically — of the High Church party, who were landed with a precious Victorian Gothic of inferior quality turned out by church furnishers, who claimed that their products were "correct"; just as the clerical outfitters, of the period invented dog-collars and other enormities of the "correctly" dressed clergyman. Craftsmen for church plate were artistically thwarted as they were allowed only to reproduce rather than create. As we have seen early in the nineteenth century they had introduced the fashionable secular shapes of goblets for communion cups and for a short time the thistle-shaped cup had a vogue; the body of the bowl often being fluted.

Butterfield in his original letter made the point that in his opinion the deep-bowled cup did not help in a reverent administration of the Sacrament. It should not be forgotten that the Sacrament was often surrounded by scenes that were, to say the least, indecorous and so the appeal to an ideal of deep religious devotion was inevitable. The pity was that the appeal was to a fictitious view of the Middle Ages. Some incidents from the ministry of Dean Hook will give a fair idea of what did happen at a celebration.

PLATE 51. (*Opposite*) Communion set, silver and silver gilt; from St Bartholomew's Church, Birmingham, 1774
height of chalice 11 in. (27.94 cm.) height of flagon 21¾ in. (55.25 cm.) diameter of paten 8½ in. (21.59 cm.)
The City of Birmingham Museum and Art Gallery, Warwickshire

PLATE 52. Chalice; 1808
height 7⅕ in. (18.30 cm.)
Cumnor, Berkshire

When Dean Hook went to Leeds in 1837, church expenses were defrayed by a church-rate which was payable by all parishioners whether members of the Established Church or not. In town parishes this led to uproarious vestry meetings at which the Dissenters would try to elect as churchwardens those who would be most likely to oppose all but the barest essential expenditure for the church and its services. At Leeds, only one churchwarden of the eight elected was a churchman. During the celebration of the Communion they sat in the vestry to "guard the wine". But the vicar had reason to suspect that they themselves occasionally consumed it. The churchwardens complained about the expense involved by the Dean's introduction of a weekly communion and by pouring away the consecrated wine which had not been used at the communion of the people.

Dean Hook wrote about such an incident to the Editor of the "British Magazine": "It so happens that in the parish church of Leeds I found the old Presbyterian way of administering the Eucharist to prevail, introduced probably at the Great Rebellion, and never since discontinued. The consecrated Elements, instead of being delivered to the communicants at the altar rails, are carried to them in the pews. From this circumstance, when there are five or six clergymen officiating, as is generally the case with us, if a sufficient quantity of wine has not been consecrated at first, it becomes difficult for the presiding priest to know how much more may be required at a second consecration. Now it so happened that on the occasion to which I am alluding, when service was over and all the people dismissed, it was discovered that in one of the cups there remained nearly half-a-pint of consecrated wine. The question then was, what was to be done with it, all the congregation being gone. The churchwardens, of whom I think five were present, demanded it as their right and offered to put it back into the bottle and keep it till the next communion. This I declined to do, because it was evidently contrary to the rubric which enjoins that the consecrated wine 'shall not be carried out of the church;' and because, knowing as I did, from the representations of the sexton, that the churchwardens were accustomed to drink some of the wine, provided for the Eucharist, in the vestry, I thought it not improbable that they might so dispose of even the consecrated Elements, for which they evidently entertained no respect." Hook goes on: "Having decided, then, not to return the consecrated wine to the churchwardens, I might have given it to the clergy who were present, but there was even then more than we could conveniently consume, and I feared that the churchwardens would have immediately written to the newspapers to attack the character of the clergy, if not exaggerate the quantity thus employed." To get over the difficulty Hook tells us that he made a hole at the side of the chancel and poured the wine away into the hole. It is then, in the light of such incidents, that the Gothic Movement should be seen; a desire to return to a halcyon past that never existed.

Victorian Plate

It was most unfortunate that the Cambridge Camden Society and its work for art in the Church was thought of as the practical side of the theology of the Tractarians. As the Tractarians became associated in the minds of many churchmen with Popery, so the Camden Society was seen in the same light. The Rev. F. Close, Vicar of Cheltenham and a most influential low churchman, in his sermon of 5th November, 1843, entitled "'The restoration of Churches' is the restoration of Popery, proved and illustrated through the authenticated publications of the Cambridge Camden Society", a sermon which sold by its thousands, his thesis was to show "That as Romanism is taught *analytically* at Oxford, it is taught *artistically* at Cambridge". Further, he makes it clear that in his opinion the re-establishment of churches, chalices and vestments in their original form is either an empty pageant or the reintroduction into England of the English churchman's great hereditary antagonistic power — POPERY. This opposition resulted in a hardening of attitude: the high churchman's mind became set and his only example of what he considered true Christian art was found in the Continental Roman Catholic churches or the designs of the Camden Society. The artist would be allowed only to elaborate the chalice shape.

Basically, of course, the desire for change was based on Eucharistic doctrine and devotion. The Camden Society wrote in April 1843 what it hoped to have for a Communion vessel, why, and what unfortunately was usually found: "Three points were indispensable in an English chalice; the bowl was always shallow and with a lip, for the convenience of draining; the base was always very broad, in order to make it stand firmly; and the stem had always a large embossed knop at the upper part, to be steadfastly grasped by the hand to prevent spilling." All these directions had their origin in that proper and necessary reverence for the consecrated Element which is often lost sight of now, hence the modern chalice has a "bowl so deep that it cannot be decently drained, a base so narrow that nothing can ensure it from falling over, and a stem so thin that there is great difficulty in taking a firm hold of it". A problem then arose, in finding examples in England which could be copied for, as yet, the work of cataloguing church plate had not begun. There was a further difficulty for them because, in their opinion, "the art of making good church plate is both lost and despised", and there was no artist who could "combine elegance and appropriate religious decoration with suitable and ecclesiastical form". But by 1846 the Cambridge Camden Society finally decided upon the shape of the chalice and the principles to be followed by all who desired to make good and correct plate. This was, of course, bound up with cost: "The beauty of good altar plate does not consist in its elegance. Elegance of metal adds nothing except weight. If, indeed, we were able to have a perfectly plain chalice and might lay out an unlimited sum on it, we should, perhaps, prefer greater weight of metal as the more valuable; but

PLATE 53. Chalice; by Henry
Wilson, 1898
*St Bartholomew's Church, Brighton
Sussex*

the money laid out on this is preferably spent on enrichments—
or on jewelry—and the like". So the way was set for the chalice illustrated (Colour Plate IV); for ordinary churches silver gilt with enamelled and pierced knop, an enamelled crucifixion on the base, in
a cheap set would cost £18, the more elaborate one about £25. The
silver gilt paten with a centre of gold work with the cruciferous nimbus
and the glory in blue, the cross in red enamel and a ruby in the initial
cross of the legend would cost about £12; unfortunately one of the
net results of this was that a great deal of Victorian plate in the medieval
style is extremely light and not as firm on its base as the Society would
have hoped.

It must be admitted, that some of the High Churchmen allowed their

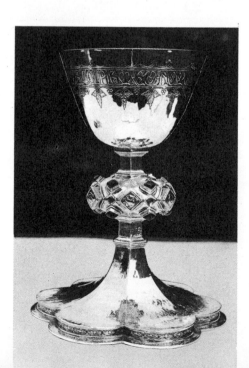

PLATE 54. Chalice, silver;
makers Omar Ramsden and
Alwyn Carr, 1910
*height 8½ in. (21.59 cm.)
Caversham Heights, Berkshire*

PLATE 55. Chalice, parcel-gilt;
designer and maker Gerald
Benney, 1958
height 12 in. (30.48 cm.)
From the modern silver collection
of The Worshipful Company of
Goldsmiths, London

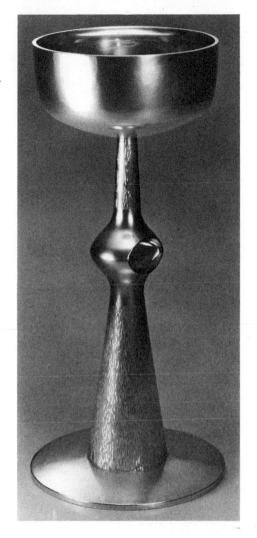

enthusiasm to become ostentation and vied with each other in the
number of jewels that could be fitted on to the chalices and the amount
of space that could be filled with enamel. But for the most part the
magnificence of these jewelled chalices is made bearable because one
knows they are the offerings by ordinary parishioners of treasured jewels
which frequently belonged to their lost loved ones. No-one could really
not love a chalice decorated with six pearls and diamonds forming the
Sacred Monogram on the base, diamonds in clusters on each lobe of the
knop and at each angle of its base, when they knew that the jewels had
been wedding presents and that a woman on her death-bed asked that

85

PLATE 56. Chalice, silver gilt; designer and maker Raymond Semple, 1964
height 7¼ in. (18.41 cm.)
The Worshipful Company of Goldsmiths, London

PLATE 57. (*Opposite*) Communion set; designer and maker John Grenville, 1961–3
height of chalice $6\frac{3}{16}$ in. (15.71 cm.) height of ciborium $5\frac{7}{8}$ in. (14.92 cm.) height of cruets $5\frac{5}{8}$ in. (14.28 cm.) length of tray 11 in. (27.94 cm.) diameter of paten $6\frac{1}{16}$ in. (15.39 cm.)
The Worshipful Company of Goldsmiths, London

they should adorn a chalice for her church. But the general church furnisher continued to use the beaker style as a basis for the cups. At Nayland, Suffolk, the cup is square with rounded corners, set on a seven inch stem, four clustered columns and a heavily moulded stepped base. This is as impractical and unaesthetic as some of the more magnificent chalices of the other cult.

Through bigotry on one side or the other, all art ceased to have any part to play in the provision of church plate. Fortunately however, art nouveau craftsmen were able to make a break-through, and at the end of the nineteenth and the beginning of the twentieth centuries artists were again able to express themselves within wide ecclesiastical limits and provide Communion vessels that reflected the artistic thought of their day. The chalice as St Bartholomew's Church, Brighton, made in 1898 by Henry Wilson (Plate 53) is, perhaps, not to present-day taste, but is the work of an artist and not a "purveyor" of church plate.

One of the most beautiful of all Gothic-style chalices, medieval or modern, is that made by Omar Ramsden in 1910 for the church of Caversham Heights, Berkshire. (Plate 54.) The irregular knop has six diamond-shaped facets with a cross engraved on one and the letters J.E.S.U.S. on the other five. The smaller facets are set with stones. The inscription around the bowl runs between decorative vine leaves. It is a little later that the magnifical silver gilt chalice at St Andrew's, Wells

86

Street, was designed by Burges, A.R.A., and made by Barkentin. Around the bowl are enamels portraying the Old Testament types of Our Lord. The stem is of malachite with enamels of the Rivers of Paradise and on the knop is the tree of life. On the base are enamels of the Crucifixion, the Virgin Mary, the Archangel Gabriel, Saint John the Evangelist and Saint Andrew, and is further decorated with a piece of fourth-century glass from the catacombs.

Church Plate 1918–1965

The period between the First and Second Great Wars was one of tremendous activity in church decoration: there was a great desire to embellish the altars in the services of the church. This, perhaps, was due to a desire to give a memorial to those who had lost their lives in the First Great War, combined with the upsurge in the high church party of the Church of England. The high church party itself, rightly taking advantage of this desire to beautify the church, was still divided between those who followed Roman Catholic taste and those who wished to see the reintroduction of the old English medieval Use of Sarum. It is not usually difficult to discover under which influence an altar was restored; the Roman influence insisted on crucifixes, six candlesticks and a tabernacle, while the Sarum Use was evidenced by an English altar — a Holy Table surrounded on three sides by curtains hung on riddell posts which were often surmounted with an angel holding a candle. As the impetus was partisan, artists were used only to accentuate party lines and so although there was tremendous activity among church furnishers, there was no resurgence of artistic expression despite the great numbers of imaginative artists at work during this time. For example the design of a candlestick which first appeared about 1902 was used with but little variation until the artist's death about 1960. This was not through lack of imagination but because of limits imposed by religious party politics. The Roman party plumped for Baroque and the Sarum party for Gothic. It was not until after the Second World War that the ecclesiastical climate allowed the craftsmen to create within the rubrical limits a recognizable Anglican style.

The artists in the post-Second War period have been supported by the interest of the Goldsmiths Company who have encouraged and supported the artist craftsman. The result has been a wonderful flowering of artists' work although as yet too many churches still refer to the well-known ecclesiastical furnishing companies who just now are searching for contemporary designs that can be reasonably produced for the church. The sound radical wind blowing through the Anglican Church bodes well for the introduction among its ornaments of contemporary artistic work of merit. One of the greatest helps to the spread of contemporary work has been Coventry Cathedral.

The communion cup designed and made by Gerald Benney in 1958 follows the Anglican tradition of the eighteenth century with its long stem which then, as now, is found to be somewhat impracticable. (Plate 55.)

The cup designed and made by Raymond Semple (Plate 56) has a feeling of the Stuart period, but is completely contemporary in its use of shapes — a cylinder, a cone and a sphere — to create an object of artistic value as well as liturgical usefulness.

The set designed and made by John Grenville in 1961 reflects the simplicity of the early medieval craftsmen with a contemporary care for proportion and ease of use. The balance of all the vessels is such that they can be used with a confidence that is not always the case. The knop on the chalice has four silver stars filled with enamel and on the base is a pietà taken from the medieval glass at Long Melford and engraved by Denis McQuoid. The knop on the ciborium has three facets, one engraved with a fish enamelled blue, another with a dove enamelled red and the third with the Manus Dei enamelled golden-yellow. (Plate 57.)

These examples are the work of but three silversmiths and we are indeed fortunate that there are working at the present time at least a dozen designer-craftsmen who are making fine contributions to our church plate in keeping with the aesthetic tenor of the twentieth century.

6 Miscellaneous Post-Reformation Plate

Inscriptions

The texts that went around the bowl of chalices are not always Eucharistic in their allusions. For example, there is a plain call for mercy on the Pallaton Chalice: "Father of Heaven have mercy upon us" (Pater de coelis miserere nobis), a suffrage from the Litany. Then on the Highworth chalice we have the quotation: "Blessed are those who hear the word of God and keep it" (Beati qui audiunt verbum dei ut custodiant illum), Saint Luke XI v. 28.

The chalice at Preston on Stour has: "I will bless the Lord at all times", Psalm 34 v. 1 (*Benedicam dñm in omni tempori*).

In the inventory of about 1400 of the Church Goods of St Martin, Ludgate, the engravings on the patens are listed, but there is no mention of any inscriptions on the chalices.

There is an interesting rebus on the Elizabethan Communion Cup now owned by Smallborough, Norfolk, but originally belonging to Hoveton. Around the bowl is inscribed: "For the towne of St Johns Hof" while the 'Ton' is shown by the drawing of a 'Tun' (a barrel).

On Elizabethan plate coats of arms usually denote that the plate was given by a donor and not bought at the parish expense. Seventeenth and eighteenth century coats of arms are frequently of great beauty.

Strangely we find on the 1616 flagon at King's Lynn: "This pott was given to God and the Church of St Margaret's, King's Linn, by Sara Cartwright, one of the daughters of Peter Cartwright, gent, one Maior, then whilst she was in her verginitie 1616".

Then by the end of the seventeenth century we again find Eucharistic allusions as a paten given at Wintersloe in 1693 had written on it "As Christ did give and make it, so receive and take it", and on a flagon at Wintersloe, also dated 1693: "Hauriat hinc populus vitam de sanguine sacro inflicto aeternus quem fulit vulnere Christus".

The inscription on a paten at Dorchester St Peter, 1684: "In their

89

superfluity of estate but for to honnour the Lord's own feast", does not give the impression of a "Widow's Mite".

On a cup at Chepstow, 1844: "The gift of a friend; prosperity to the Church of England", alludes to the encroachments threatened to the establishment by the reforming zeal of the Whigs.

Many inscriptions on nineteenth-century plate presented to the Church are very simple, such as: "A humble thank-offering on recovery from sickness".

Often donors of plate inscribed their names and coats of arms, but it must be admitted that sometimes they had: "commendable modesty not to herald the fact by any inscription".

On the Okeford Fitzpaine, Dorset, flagon, which was given by Mrs Joan Baker in 1684, is inscribed: "To be by them us'd onely in the' sacrament of the Lord's Supper". This request might seem to be self-evident but there are many indications that vestry meetings at times were very convivial affairs and the donor was wishing to avoid the use of her flagon for a secular party, such as must have been held at Parham in Suffolk, where there is a lemon squeezer given to the vestry in the eighteenth century to be used in making the punch to keep the vestry meeting in good heart.

Then on a late nineteenth-century paten at Netherbury, Dorset, is written: "The money offered at Churching of Women during the vicariate of H.W.Y. purchased this paten for the service of God". This refers to the Rubric at the end of the service of Churching which states that the woman must produce accustomed offerings which were, and sometimes still are, though infrequently, a gift to the parson.

Up to the time of the repeal of the church rate which provided for the upkeep of the parish church, alms were taken only for charitable purposes and not, as now, for all that comes under the heading of church expenses. The former practice is shown by the inscriptions on many alms bowls such as: "Blessed be the man that provideth for the sick and needy" (Psalm 91); or "He that hath pity upon the poor lendeth unto the Lord" (Proverbs).

It is frequently the case that benefactions to churches and the poor of the parish are written on boards hung in the church. Frederick Burgess, in his "English Churchyard Memorials", notes that a tablet in the church at Wainfleet, Lincolnshire, to Edward Barkham, 1735, records among his gifts to the church two large flagons, a chalice with a cover together with a paten, all of silverplate. At Bucklebury, Berkshire, we find, however, the silver itself noted: "1712, Rev. Symeon, Vicar, gave a silver cup and cover to the value of £4 10s. 0d. for the service of Holy Communion, which had since been re-cast, at the charge of our Rev. Wickham Henry Howard Hartley, the present vicar, into a silver plate to the value of £11 9s. 7d. Mr. Hartley gave this alms dish in 1824". "1812, also a silver flagon, chalice of gilt and paten: £32,: Rev. W. H. H. Hartley, Lord of this manor and Vicar".

Exchange of Plate

The Victorians have been castigated by almost every writer on church plate for their habit of exchanging, disposing or selling "old" plate for "new". It is true that many of the new vessels which they bought were plated and indeed of poor design, almost always the silversmith's idea of what a gothic chalice was like. The Cambridge Camden Society was always inveighing against the employment of uneducated goldsmiths for this purpose; they were as keen as anybody for the changing of everything into Gothic. It must be remembered though that Gothic was for many people the only permissable art for a Christian, all other art being pagan, and thus, one should have a certain sympathy for the parsons and churchwardens who disposed of the old to instil a Christian feeling into their flocks; also some of the plate had, no doubt, become battered and worn. The Rector of Halstock in Dorset sold the Elizabethan cup and cover which was in a poor state for about 30s., and bought, at his own expense, a copy of the medieval chalice and paten at Trinity College, Oxford, as was recommended by the Camden Society — the chalice having been illustrated in their "Instrumenta Ecclesiastica".

This habit of selling or re-using old plate has always been present in the minds of parsons and churchwardens. In 1686, at Sowerby, the old plate was exchanged for something more to the artistic taste of the age, and Sir Thomas Aubrey, in the terms of his gift of plate on 26th January, 1637, to Llantarthye churchwardens wrote: "with power to exchange it for one of another fashion when desirable". Also, there is the incident of a flagon of 1597, weighing twenty-nine and three quarter ounces, and a flagon of 1682, weighing fifty-five and a half ounces, that were re-made into one flagon in 1867 of over eighty ounces.

Another aspect of this changing of silver for plated vessels is shown by the behaviour of Archdeacon Doubeney who was Vicar at North Bradley, Wiltshire, from 1778 to 1827, who said, when he was dangerously ill on one occasion: "Let the Communion vessels be plated. I have always condemned those who have placed unnecessary temptations in the path of their fellow men and I am anxious that the last act of my life should hold out to others no inducement to sin". The Archdeacon who built the church at Rodehill presented it with a full set of plated vessels.

Thefts from churches must have been frequent even from early ages for in 601 Gregory the Great replied to Saint Augustine of Canterbury's question, "What punishment must be inflicted if anyone shall take anything by theft from the Church" with "The motive of the thief be distinguished and the punishment, either fine or stripes, to be governed by charity not passion".

There is an interesting account of theft from the Warden's accounts of the Parish of Morbath, Devon, transcribed by the Rev. J. Erskine Binney, 1904: "The stealing of the chalice of this Church in the year 1534. On the 20th November, it was the Feast of St Edmund, King and Martyr; it was upon the Friday between the Friday and the Saturday;

the thief with a ladder got up upon the Church and pulled up the ladder after him and set the ladder to the Tower window and broke open the window and so got into the bells and from the bells got down into the Church, and with a firebox struck fire which he left behind him. Then broke open the stock chest and the other great chest and took away the chalice that was in the Stock chest, and St Sidwell's shoe of silver and nothing else, and so got out of the choir door and shut it after him.

Upon this the young men and maidens of the Parish got together and with their gifts bought another chalice without any charge to the Parish. The new chalice was six and a half ounces and cost 38s. 8d., 4d. more to have it blessed and 1s. for their expenses."

The Safe Custody of Plate

In 1756 the church plate at Broad Hinton was stolen. After advertisements offering a reward were unsuccessful the church wardens consulted a "cunning man" who lived at Corsham. He was to bring his wand and douse for the metal which was thought to be still concealed in the village. The "cunning man" suggested that they should give notice that the chancel door and chest would be left open for three nights and if the plate was not returned during that time, the douser would come and discover the thief. As the plate lost is now in the possession of the church this ruse would appear to have been successful.

At Garsden in Wiltshire a box containing valuable plate was lost sight of and in 1822 its adventures were described in a letter written by the Rev. J. H. Newbury: "The plate for many years had been kept in a box and desposited in a lumber closet in the old mansion. There was an idle story in the village that a ghost had formerly been laid in the box; a story that perhaps was useful as a double lock for a superstitious dread of describing the ghost factually deterred many from indulging their curiosity by looking into it. Having understood from an old man that there was some Communion Plate at the great house, the clergyman made enquiries, and to the utter surprise of the people of the house, upon opening the lid of the box (for the first time, perhaps, for a century) instead of seeing a ghost jump out, this valuable service of tarnished plate presented itself and was immediately taken to the vicarage house".

This habit of keeping church plate at the rectory or vicarage has led, on occasions, to plate being lost on the sudden decease of the incumbent; plate found in the house has been considered to be his property and there are many examples of it taking some years before restitution has been made. Similarly this is the case when plate was kept in the plate room at the big house.

PLATE V. Verger's Staff, ebonised beech, gold plate and silver; designed and made by Gerald Benney
length 42 in. (106.68 cm.). Coventry Cathedral, Warwickshire

In the same way ignorance of silver marks has led to the loss of Britannia standard plate. These marks have sometimes been mistaken for those used by pewterers and the vessels so marked being thought to be "only pewter" have been left unguarded.

The accounts of the great monastic houses show that they pledged their plate to Jews for ready cash — a practice which led to the encouragement of anti-Semitism by the monks. Occasionally one also finds records of parish churches pawning their plate, usually to raise money to put into good repair the church or, perhaps, the property belonging to the church. It must be remembered that with the rise of the movement to have Masses said specifically for personal benefit, the cost to the church would have to be guaranteed by the person seeking such benefits. It was laid down that each chantry priest should be paid a specific sum per annum. This was paid by the income derived from property left for that specific purpose.

Flagons

The most impressive pieces of church plate are the flagons, especially when seen amidst other altar plate standing on the altar for display at the great festivals of the Church.

The amount of wine needed at the pre-Reformation Mass was small since only the priest communicated and the cruet was sufficient for many celebrations, but with the restoration of the cup to the laity more wine was needed for the celebration and Communion of the people.

Oman in his "English Church Plate" refers to flagons in two city churches during the reign of Edward VI, but these are exceptional; the earliest surviving flagon, dated 1572, is at Wells Cathedral. Although, until the eighteenth century, flagons were usually cylindrical, there are a pair with a 1577 hall-mark at Cirencester (Plate 58), one weighing sixty-six ounces and the other sixty-seven ounces, which are pot-bellied with long cylindrical necks standing on a foot, and whose covers are engraved with "Villa Cirencistrie 1577" and a view of a town. There are, however, a number of Elizabethan domestic flagons, at Charsfield in Suffolk and Crosthwaite in Norfolk, which would seem to have been given by a family in the parish in obedience to the canons of 1603 which ordered that the wine be brought to the Communion Table in a "clean, sweet standing pot or stoup of pewter if not of purer metal". It is from this date that we find numerous gifts and purchases of flagons in connection with parish churches.

The need for large quantities of wine has sometimes been questioned, but from Archdeacons' visitations when parishioners were presented for not communicating it would appear that partaking of the sacrament

PLATE VI. The Canterbury Cross, silver gilt
height 84 in. (213.36 cm.) width 8½ in. (21.59 cm.). Lambeth Palace, London

PLATE 58. Flagon; maker's mark
RH in monogram over a pallet,
1577
height 13½ in. (35.29 cm.)
Cirencester, Gloucestershire

had become a matter of necessity if one were to avoid coming into collision with ecclesiastical discipline; thus, in a Kent parish of a hundred and twenty houses there were four hundred communicants and in another parish of sixty-two houses there were one hundred communicants. It is true that the amount of wine that the flagons can hold is great. For example there are five flagons at St Margaret's, King's Lynn, given between the years 1615 and 1639, which weigh between sixty ounces and seventy-two ounces and it has been calculated that these would hold roughly one and a half gallons of wine. One can but presume that

94

it was the custom to take a pull at the cup and not a sip—a custom which still survives among some communicants. This is borne out by the church accounts of Gawsworth when a change of habit in the nineteenth century is noted: in 1853 over six Sacrament Sundays twelve bottles were consumed at a total cost of £4 9s. 3d. In 1859 there were seven Sacraments during the year and the amount expended on wine £7 13s. 10½d. However, when a reforming clergyman took over the provision of the wine in 1868, there were twelve Sacrament Sundays and the total cost of the wine came to only £1 16s. 0d. This may be, of course, because there were fewer communicants but at the same time the reverence for the Sacrament was leading people to take but a small sip at the cup.

There were, however, other reasons that led to the flagons being filled with wine. There was an interpretation of the Rubric at the end of the Communion Service which said that if any of the bread or wine remained the curate should have it to his own use. The point of this Rubric was not to give the parson whatever might remain of the consecrated bread and wine after the Communion of the people, but what remained from the unconsecrated bread and wine. Puritans had taken advantage since the Rubric of the 1552 prayer book to take home and use as common food any of the consecrated bread and wine which had remained, but in the 1661 Rubric the word "unconsecratia" was added to prevent this profanation. There seemed to be relics of this arrangement in some

PLATE 59. Flagon, silver gilt; maker's mark *hound sejant*, 1655 *height 10 in. (25.4 cm.) Staunton Harold, Leicestershire*

95

PLATE 60. Flagon, silver; hall-marks: *Old English N in a square shield, lion passant in a plain oblong, leopard's head crowned in a pounded shield, F.B.N.D. on a plain square*(the marks of François Butler and Nich. Dumée), *sacred monogram on the bowl with a cross and three nails within a circle of glory, arms of Sir John Clobury of Wentworth impaling those of his wife,* dated 1768 *height 14 in. (35.56 cm.) diameter of base 5½ in. (13.97 cm.) Church of All Saints, Kirkby Mallory, Leicestershire*

churches where an agreement was made that the parson should have a bottle of wine for his own use at the expense of the parish each time there was a Communion Service. An extraordinary continuance of this custom was, as we have seen, found by Dean Hook at Leeds in 1842.

Some people have wondered at the cylindrical flagons as at Staunton Harold, Leicestershire, (Plate 59) without a spout or lip as being very difficult and indeed clumsy to pour from, but experience has shown that this is not so, and so for most churches an ordinary tankard was duly provided to obey the canon of 1603. The shape of these follows closely that of the tankards in secular use. In the eighteenth century the coffee-pot style, mixed with the cylindrical and bulbous flagon, was very popular, and at the end of the century there were whole sets of altar furniture in Adams style with the flagons taking every conceivable form of ewer shape. In the 1840's the Camden Society, in its "Instrumenta Ecclesiastica" gives two examples which it recommends; one based on the Guille cruet at Guernsey (Plate 14) and the other of similar shape but with a lip at the top of the neck rather than a spout from the centre

PLATE 61. Flagon, silver gilt;
maker's mark *Paul Storr*, 1821
height 18 in. (45.72 cm.)
St Pancras' Church, London

of the belly. They were not in favour of large flagons but preferred that there should be two moderate sized ones which they thought to be more beautiful and convenient. Large flagons for sacramental use have not been made for the last hundred years or more since there are fewer communicants who consume less wine for the reasons already suggested.

It is of interest to note that there are many more pewter flagons than silver ones in churches, mostly dating from the end of the seventeenth and beginning of the eighteenth centuries when Archdeacons made a drive to implement the 1603 canon. It is indeed a pity that few parishes nowadays ever see their silver flagons which are kept safely in the bank or church chest. The most frequent article of church plate for which a faculty is sought to be disposed of is the flagon, but when people realize that it has been used in the Sacrament itself and not just as a container of wine they can understand that disposal of it for profane use is not a happy thought, for the rubric directs that in the consecration prayer "the priest is to lay his hand upon every vessel (be it chalice or flagon) in which there is any wine to be consecrated".

97

The eighteenth century found the coffee-pot style extremely popular as shown in Plate 60, the flagon at All Saints, Kirkby Mallory, Leicestershire; while a truly magnifical style coffee-pot flagon was produced by Paul Storr (Plate 61) for the Grecian style church of St Pancras, London.

Alms Basins

In the 1662 Prayer Book the rubric after the Offertory sentence in the Communion Service directs that the alms of the people should be collected in a "decent bason". In the earlier Prayer Books the rubric had directed that the alms should be put either directly into the poor box or collected and then put into the poor box. No reference was made to any collecting bowl and it was only from the Restoration that alms bowls were found in the churches. That illustrated (Plate 62), from

PLATE 62. Alms dish, silver gilt; maker's mark *P.R. in cypher*, 1685 *diameter 25 in. (63.5 cm.). Westminster Abbey, London*

PLATE 63. Alms dish, silver ; maker's mark *MW in monogram*, London 1650 diameter 13¾ in. (34.92 cm.). On loan to The Royal Scottish Museum, Edinburgh from a private collection

Westminster Abbey, is truly magnificent, and that in the Royal Scottish Museum (Plate 63) shows that many cathedrals and large parish churches possessed a bowl both decent and in good taste. For the most part the parishes provided small plates or the "marriage plates", of the late seventeenth century, given by widows, and often decorated with beautiful coats of arms on the border.

Other seventeenth-century articles often given were sweetmeat dishes with two handles.

In the eighteenth century the collecting shoe makes its appearance. (Plate 64.) Sometimes these had their bowls half covered so that it was not possible to see what had been put in. The Victorians desired that every picture should tell a story; that from Bradfield, Berkshire (Plate 65) illustrated the story of the widow's mite. They are now usually brass.

It is interesting that these bowls were displayed on the Holy Table in the seventeenth and eighteenth centuries and by the mid-nineteenth century they were placed in the centre of the Holy Table to demonstrate the church's sound Protestant churchmanship in opposition to the cross found on the altar of the more Catholic-minded parson. The writer well remembers Bishop Donaldson turning dramatically towards the Holy Table at the end of a magnificent peroration and pointing to "the symbol of your faith": this he thought to be a cross but discovered it was an alms bowl.

It should be remembered that in medieval days there were dues payable to the parish priest. It is said that the word "oblations" in the prayer for the church militant refers to this and in some inventories and wills there are references to dishes for such offerings. Some are made of copper and others silver. Sir John Percyvale left to St Mary Woolnoth in London in the sixteenth century two parcel gilt basons weighing one hundred and twenty-two ounces: "In the botom whereof the Holy Name of IHŪ is graven to the intent that the same basons to the lawde parysing and honour of Almighty God shall serve and be set forth upon the High Awlter in times and feasts convenient for

99

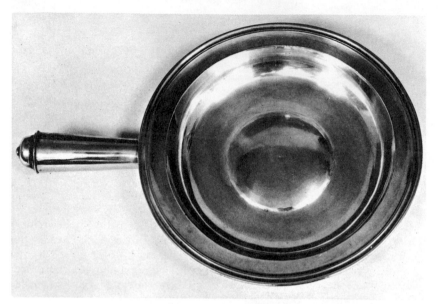

PLATE 64. Collecting shoe, silver; maker's mark *RG TG* for Richard Gurney & Co., 1747
length 14⅞ in. (37.78 cm.) diameter 10½ in. (26.67 cm.) Norwell, Nottinghamshire

evermore, and to be occupied at such times and feasts convenient for to receive only the offerings there to be made". These basons would seem, however, to be the exception rather than the rule.

Staves
The Verger's Staff of the seventeenth and eighteenth century is a rod, surmounted with a figure or device, carried as an emblem of authority. Many of these are instances of beautiful and elaborate design and workmanship. The Beadle, who carried the verge, was one who called and attended the Parish Meetings, in fact in the ancient Anglo-Saxon version of the New Testament we find the word "beadle" used in the text Saint Luke XII.58: "... Lest he haul thee to the Judge and the Judge deliver thee to the Beadle." The Beadle was also frequently, in the seventeenth century, the Constable of the Parish. Another definition of beadle is a lay officer who preserves order in churches or chapels; the officer who, on public occasions, bears the verge or staff of office before the Bishop, Dean, Canon or other dignitary or ecclesiastic. The verge is a staff of wood or metal surmounted with a figure, emblem or device, borne before the Bishop, Dean, Rector or Vicar on entering or leaving church or on other public occasions. In the old English Sarum rite, the Verger headed the procession.

100

PLATE 65. Alms dish, silver;
makers Roly and Storer, 1843
diameter 9¼ in. (24.76 cm.)
St Andrew's Church, Bradfield,
Berkshire

The beadle portrayed in Hogarth's drawings of the Idle Apprentice at play in the Churchyard during Divine Service is about to beat the boys with his staff.

As Mr Toulmin Smith says, the beadle is an officer whose existence is the proof of the fact and long practice of active local self-government; the beadle would accompany the parish officials with the clergy and school children in the perambulation of the parish to mark the boundaries. One of the few remaining active beadles is still to be found in Westminster Abbey. The vast majority of beadles' staves are to be found in the churches of London, the earliest at Chadwell of 1683.

Churchwardens have their staves and the difference between the People's and Incumbent's Churchwarden is usually signified by the People's Churchwarden having a crown surmounting his staff and the Incumbent's a mitre.

The beadle's staff of St Dunstan, Stepney is crowned with a medallion of silver, on one side the Tower of London in repoussé (Plate 66) and on the other a ship in full sail. Mostly, however, Vergers' and beadles' staves were surmounted with the emblems representing the saint of the dedication of the church; for example St Clement would be represented with an anchor; a church dedicated to St George with a representation of St George killing the dragon; Poplar, with the dock gates surmounted

PLATE 66. Beadle's staff, silver medallion; 1784
St Dunstan's Church, Stepney, London

by a ship; and St Margaret's, Westminster with Saint Margaret of Antioch standing on the dragon from which she has just emerged. This topicality is still illustrated by the Verger's Staff made by Gerald Benney for Coventry Cathedral. (Colour Plate V). This Verger's Staff is topped with the Coventry Cross of nails between two maple leaves, the emblem of Canada. This will be a permanent reminder of what Canadians had to do with the restoration of the cathedral; in fact Canadian organists contributed a large sum of money toward the building of the Cathedral organ.

Dr Reginald Eager, in 1897 writes: "The writer, from boyhood, both in London City and country churches, remembers vergers in their black robes barred with velvet and tassels on the sleeves, perhaps adorned with a silver badge and carrying a silver or gold mace or rod or wooden verge with a metal badge on the top. At St Mary the Virgin, Guildford, the verger and parish clerk both had such habits and the clerk carried a fine silver mace. Old gowns are still used by the verger and sexton in the Parish Church of St Peter and St Paul, Frampton

102

Cotterill and the verger carries a verge with a silver top". This is but seldom seen: for alas the race of parish clerks is slowly dying out.

It would seem that some cathedrals have staves dating from the Restoration; that at Norwich, dated 1660, is carried before the Bishop in the Cathedral, and sometimes when he is officiating in the churches of his Diocese. Also the two staves of two feet, nine inches each, surmounted by a dove, are dated 1660 by the inscription IN CONVERTENDO CAPTIVITATEM SION 1660. They still form part of the Verger's equipment to be seen in use at every Cathedral service.

Font Basins

The font was placed near the church door to signify the Christian's entrance into God's church by baptism, but the Reformers noticed that in large churches the congregation was unable to see what was going on at the font, so many of them suggested the use of a portable font, or at any rate, a small font basin attached to the pulpit or altar rails. This would facilitate the baptism taking place in the sight of the whole congregation. The high churchmen, however, it must be remembered, objected to this and in 1604 ordered the font to be kept in its usual place. At the Restoration in 1661, when the question was again raised, the matter was left open and nothing was stated about the position of the font.

PLATE 67. Christening Font and Alms Bason; 1740
diameter 10½ in. (26.67 cm.). St Michael's Church, Basingstoke, Hampshire

So it came about that in many churches a small font basin was introduced, fitting into a bracket on the altar rails or the altar, or set up in front of the pulpit. The "Ecclesiologist" quotes of St George's, Hanover Square: "The font is unique in form and situation. It resembles a tolerably sized marble wine cooler, fixed in a circular carved oak frame about a foot high, the whole machine runs upon castors and is wheeled out when wanted from under the Communion Table".

It might well be said that the inconvenience of a congregation turning round towards the font at the west end of the church has led largely to baptisms becoming a private service for a family, rather than an occasion for the whole congregation.

There was a bowl given in 1730 to St Michael's Basingstoke. (Plate 67.)

PLATE 68. Christening Font of Charles II, silver gilt; 1660
height 37 in. (93.98 cm.)
The Tower of London

Its diameter was ten and a half inches and the centre of the bowl was engraved with large figures of Saint Michael and the dragon. The inscription makes it clear that his bowl was intended both as a font and also as an alms basin.

Among the Crown Jewels at the Tower of London is a silver gilt font and basin (Plate 68) made in 1660. The son of James II (the "warming-pan baby") is the first royal baby recorded as having had this font used for his christening. It has not been used since the christening of George III's children.

Primatial Crosses

The Archiepiscopal Cross appears in the hand of Gregory the Great in the diptych of Monza (510). It was carried before the Pope in outdoor processions in the eighth century and would seem to have been part of the equipment of metropolitans of that century; it was certainly used by Egbert, Archbishop of York, whose brother, Eadberht, was King of Northumbria and who, as Oman in "The Coinage of England" (p. 14) says, "From fraternal affection or gratitude struck a *sceat* with his own usual obverse but with, on the reverse, his brother's figure standing with mitre and cross".

By the Middle Ages it had certainly become a symbol of jurisdiction and fierce were the battles between the Archbishops of Canterbury and York for precedence. In 1280 William de Wickwaine, Archbishop of York, wrote to the Pope: "Adam de Hales, an officer of my Lord of Canterbury, rushed like a madman upon my attendants and scandalously broke my cross in pieces: but thanks be to God, I soon caused another to be raised and carried. Moreover, most holy father, when I am journeying through the province of Canterbury on business relating to my own see, my Lord of Canterbury forbids food or lodging to be supplied to myself or my attendants on pain of excommunication exactly as if we were heretics and places the whole district where I make any sojourn under an ecclesiastical interdict".

The precedence was eventually conceded to Canterbury. The cross was carried before the Archbishop, who, like other bishops, carried his episcopal staff.

The Primatial Cross shown in Hans Holbein, the Younger's picture of Archbishop Warham in the Musée du Louvre, dated 1527, shows an elaborately enamelled crucifix on his coat of arms, at the foot, and mitre. This one would seem to have been his own personal property made specially for him.

But Archbishop Cranmer, however, painted by Fliccieus, has only Renaissance wooden carved caryiated monsters flanking the window in front of which he sits, with no primatial staff.

Its use went out at the Reformation, but like the staff was not forgotten entirely as it is shown on the monument of Archbishop William of York (died 1650) at Llandegai and of Archbishop Lamplugh (died 1691) at

York. It was not used again until 1883 when the present Cross—popularly called the Cross of Canterbury—was presented to Archbishop Benson for him and his successors in the see by the clergy of the Province of Canterbury upon his translation from the see of Truro to that of Canterbury. The Cross was made by Messrs Hardman of Birmingham under the general direction of Messrs Bodley and Garner. (Colour Plate VI.)

The figures in the lower tier represent Saint Matthew, Saint Mark, Saint John and Saint Luke, Saint Peter and Saint Paul. In the upper tier are the figures of Saint Augustine—the apostle of the English and first Archbishop of Canterbury—Saint Virgilius, Archbishop of Arles, from whom Saint Augustine received episcopal consecration, Saint Theodore of Tarsus, 7th Archbishop of Canterbury, Saint Hugh, Bishop of Lincoln, Saint Piran and Saint Petroc, missionaries to Cornwall. It is silver gilt and six feet high. Into the original cross there have been inserted three sapphires from the state collection of Brisbane and three opals from the Diocese of Sydney, presented to Archbishop Fisher when he visited Australia in 1950.

Croziers

It has been suggested that the vestments and ornaments of Christian bishops derived from those of Roman Consuls. If that is so, then the pastoral staff would have been the *scipio eburneus,* a short staff about the length of a modern walking stick. There is, of course, evidence that by the fifth century at least the staff was part of a bishop's regalia, and Saint Isidore of Seville tells us, in the seventh century, of bishops receiving their staff at their consecration.

There is an early staff of the seventh century preserved which is of wood covered with silver.

In the early Christian iconography it is frequently to be seen that Jesus is carrying a wand as he performs His miracles and so it is easy to see why the wand should be part, as we have said, of the bishops' uniform. The next variety of staff that made its appearance is one which has its head in the shape of the Greek letter "Tau". This could well have been used as a crutch for support when preaching in the open air. Gradually the end was curved and so took on the appearance of a shepherd's crook. Many of those belonging to well-known Celtic missionary saints were held in great reverence, particularly by the Scots, and after the death of the saint they were covered with gold, silver and copper. It has been suggested that there was no pastoral significance in the staff with its curved top having the appearance of a shepherd's crook, but there is the saying: "The crook leads the gentle, the sharp point pricks the proud"; or again "The shepherd's staff, by its own straightness, signifies a strict rule of life, the curved end takes charge of the down-trodden while the sharp end subdues the proud".

The pastoral staff found in the grave of Bishop Grosseteste (died

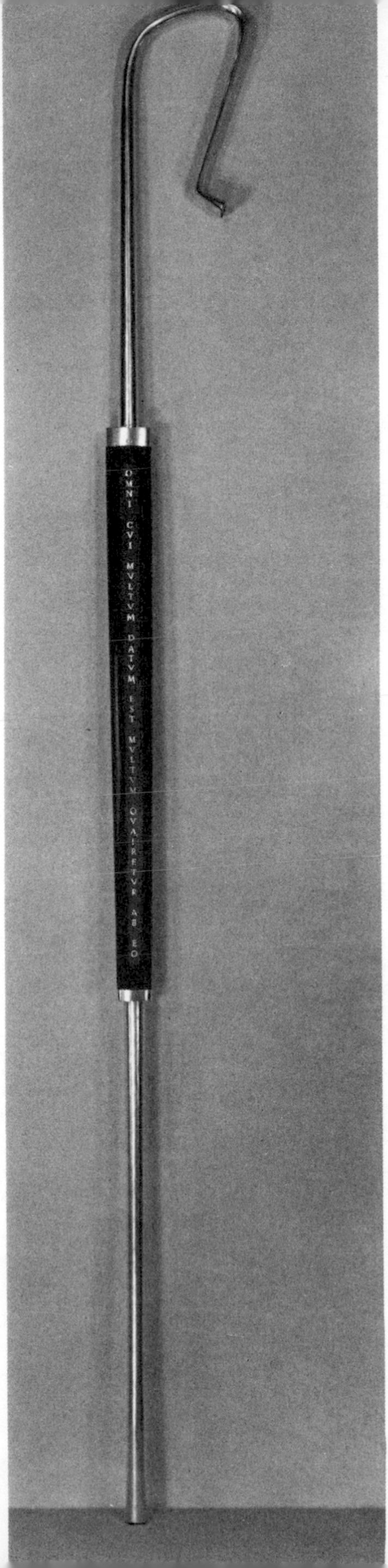

PLATE 69. Pastoral Staff, gold
and silver with an ebony staff
and an inscription inlaid in
gold; designer and maker Gerald
Benney, 1959
length 66 in. (167.64 cm.)
Presented to the Rt. Rev. J.R.H.
Moorman, on his appointment as
Bishop of Ripon, by the old
students of Chichester Theological
College of which he was
formerly Principal

1253) has on its collar: "PER BACULI FORMAM: PRAELATI DISCITO NORMAM", which may be translated: "By the shape of the staff learn the pattern of the Bishop". There would, therefore, seem to be no grounds for suggesting that the pastoral staff is not the staff of a shepherd of his flock.

By the early Middle Ages the staff was given to the episcopal candidate with the words: "Receive the staff of the pastoral office" (*Baculum pastoralitatis*). Only much later did it become an insignia of jurisdiction to be carried by the bishop, and then only in his own diocese; indeed until recently some Anglican prelates denied bishops from other dioceses the use of their pastoral staffs. Some other Anglican prelates regard it as an ornament as if it were a mace or staff and have it carried in front of them by a chaplain instead of walking with it held in the left hand. They are confusing their pastoral staff with the Primatial Cross.

An interesting piece of evidence of the crozier being the symbol of authority may be derived from Foxe's description of the degradation of Archbishop Cranmer: "To take from him his crozier staff out of his hand which he held fast and refused to deliver."

Archbishop Lang revived the proper use for a primate in holding his own pastoral staff as he walked while a chaplain went before him bearing the Primatial Cross, which is indeed a mace and not a cross, although some of his more immediate predecessors had regarded the primatial cross as an archiepiscopal substitute for the pastoral staff.

Bishop Fox's crozier (Colour Plate VII) is only slightly enamelled but the magnificent Wykeham Crozier left to New College, Oxford, in 1403 has translucent enamels which are glorious in their colour and are, without doubt, of English origin. Also beautiful is the Limerick Pastoral Staff with its magnificent Annunciation in the crook, its leaves and canopied saints, and which is inscribed "Thomas O'Carty artifex faciam".

An excellent example of a contemporary pastoral staff is that given to Rt Rev. J. R. H. Moorman on his appointment as Bishop of Ripon, by the old students of Chichester Theological College, of which he was formerly principal It was made by Gerald Benney in 1959. (Plate 69.)

Rings
In early days, when bishops were appointed by the King, the King delivered a ring and pastoral staff to a priest. This became through the ages a matter of contention between the King and the Papacy, but when the authority of the Papacy over the Church of England was repudiated by Henry VIII the problem ceased to be of any importance and from the Reformation the reformed ceremonies of election and consecration omitted all reference to rings and pastoral staffs.

PLATE VII. The Corpus Christi Crozier
height 71¼ in. (180.9 cm.), Corpus Christi College, Oxford

Rings, from the earliest days have been a token of authority. Pharaoh took off his signet ring and put it upon Joseph's hand (Genesis 41 v.42) and Ahasuerus took his ring from his hand and gave it unto Haman (Esther 3 v. 10). Although rings have been worn by all kinds of people from the earliest days, by the seventh century a ring was given to a bishop at his consecration together with his staff to show his authority and responsibility. The ring was worn on the middle finger of the right hand; later it was put onto the fourth finger of the right hand. Several rings have been found in the tombs of bishops. Saint Virinus' ring was found when his grave was opened in the thirteenth century at Dorchester upon Thame, and many other rings have been found when bishops' graves have been opened. Bishops frequently left their pontifical rings to their successors, but this custom ceased at the Reformation.

The use of rings among bishops of the Church of England has now been generally restored.

Pectoral Cross
In a company of clergy, some of whom may be bishops and others archdeacons, all dressed in the old-fashioned way of apron and gaiters, one could, at the present time, distinguish the bishop from the archdeacon by the pectoral cross he wears.

In early Christian days, and indeed today, the pectoral cross could be worn by all Christians who so wished, but prelates, from the earliest days, have worn pectoral crosses of special value. However, no traces of pectoral crosses belonging to pre-Reformation Anglican bishops have been found as part of their official dress, although there are the crosses found in the graves of Saint Cuthbert, 686, at Durham and Saint Alphege, 1082. These would, therefore, appear to be personal ornaments.

In the Middle Ages bishops, like others, would no doubt wear pectoral crosses as a reliquary containing a portion of the True Cross, but not today; so we are now in a position where the most obvious distinguishing mark of an Anglican bishop is a personal ornament, for which there is no authority as a liturgical ornament. Be this as it may, the beauty of many of the pectoral crosses and their association with former bishops who have handed them down now invests the bishop's pectoral cross with both interest, point and beauty.

The artist is enabled, by freedom from all limitation but size, to exercise great ingenuity and imagination in the use of material and association; for example a bishop with Scottish associations has a beautiful chased pectoral cross in the form of a Celtic Cross; another with connections with the Franciscan Order has a silver cross daintily chased with a crucifix and enamelled with red and gold.

PLATE VIII. Sir Peter Glean's Cup
height 16 in. (40.6 cm.), St Peter Mancroft, Norwich, Norfolk

The Cuthbert Cross is regarded by Kendrick as fifth century and a work of the early Christian Church. Although we call it a Pectoral Cross and think that it was worn by Saint Cuthbert in everyday use it may, however, as Kendrick suggests, have been placed on his breast and about his neck in the grave. There is, of course, the Wilton pectoral cross which was made by the goldsmith of the Sutton Hoo treasure.

It is interesting to see how effective the design of the Cuthbert Cross is when amended to be a processional cross, as was done by John Gray who designed the processional cross for St Albans Copnor, Portsmouth, which was made by Leslie Durbin.

Flower Decoration of Churches
From the earliest days it has been the custom to have flowers in Church and Saint Augustine mentions flowers being taken to the bedside of a dying man—flowers that had been on the Altar. (It is a custom of Indian Christians to make chains of flowers on their way to Church and on their entrance to take their flowers and place them on the Altar.) But it does not seem that vases especially for flowers were used until the middle of the nineteenth century, when it was still the custom of both peasants and gentle folk to take small bunches of flowers in the hand to Church.

From the early sixteenth century there are records of churches being decorated for the great feasts. In the accounts of St Mary at Hill in the City of London there is: "holme and ivy for Christmas Eve, 4d."; then in 1647, in the accounts of St Margaret's, Westminster: "Paid for rosemary and bayes that were stuck about the Church at Christmas, 1s 6d". Herbert, in his "Country Parson", 1652, said: "Our parson ordered that the church be swept and kept clean without dust or cobwebs, and at great festivals strewed and stuck with boughs;" but it is obvious from the decorations mentioned that it was a dressing up of the Church rather than the providing of vases and flowers.

In 1882, Mr Geldart edited a book by Mr Cox, who was a provider of ecclesiastical bric-à-brac, and gives lists of the flowers to be used for the various months of the year, showing in his illustrations decanter and pear-shaped vases of brass. In general though, it was the decoration of pillars, fonts, pulpits, altar rails and other furniture which gained the attention of the ladies of the village, and it is only in recent years that the shape of vases in precious metals have been used. Frequently flower vases are made *en suite* with cross and candlesticks and wide-mouthed vases instead of carafe and pear-shaped ones.

Gifts of Secular Plate
The simplicity and, in many cases, poverty of the church plate of Elizabethan days contrasted with the splendid plate in the halls of the county and merchant families. So it is we find that the church possesses the most wonderful collection of secular plate of the sixteenth and seventeenth
110

PLATE 70. Tazze; (*right*) maker's
mark *W.G.*, London 1679
height 4¾ in. (12.06 cm.)
diameter 6 in. (15.24 cm.)
(*left*) maker S. Gilbert, Ipswich,
circa 1570
height 4½ in. (11.43 cm.)
diameter 7 in. (17.78 cm.)
Charsfield Church, Suffolk

centuries. For example, the Sir Peter Gleane cup and cover given to
St Peter Mancroft Church, Norwich in 1633 (Colour Plate VIII) is
one of the most magnificent cups remaining of its period. It was made
in 1625. Around the bowl King David is accepting gifts from Abigail,
who is followed by a train of ladies, servants, camels and asses, while
the cover has three subjects: David sending messengers to Nabal; the
messengers reception and their return.

One of the most common of the gifts to churches was standing tazze
for use as ciborium. The Church at Charsfield Suffolk has two (Plate 70).
One made about 1580 has the Wingfield monogram in the centre and
the other is of 1679. These, together with an Elizabethan ewer-shaped
flagon with the date 1576 and the Wingfield arms on the lid, were
probably given towards the last quarter of the seventeenth century.

Another gift of this period by one of the Bacon family to Redgrave
Church, Suffolk, is a cover to a thistle-shaped chalice. The cover is the
salt and spice box that belonged to a secular salt, but which by some
mistake was given to the church.

Engraving on Vessels

Usually, to denote a holy use, the vessels were engraved with the
Sacred Monogram amidst the rays of glory, as on the chalice of Norbury.
(Plate 48.) This was originally the mark of the Jesuits at the time of the
Counter-Reformation, but it found its way quite happily on to English
plate.

Sometimes one finds the vessels engraved with scenes from Our
Lord's Passion. The cup, paten and flagon at Henley, Suffolk (Plates
71 and 72) have the engravings of the Crucifixion, the Last Supper and
the Scourging of Our Lord, but such engravings are rare.

Communion of the Sick, Post-Reformation

We have seen in the Middle Ages that the sick and dying were assured
of the Sacrament at the shortest notice from that reserved in the church,
and that when circumstances demanded a celebration other than in a
church, stringent conditions laid down by the bishop had to be fulfilled.

111

PLATE 71. Chalice engraved with a scene of the Crucifixion, Paten engraved
with a scene of The Last Supper, and Flagon engraved with a scene of the
Scourging of Jesus; maker Edward Pocock, London 1728
height of chalice 7¼ in. (18.41 cm.) diameter of paten 5⅝ in. (14.28 cm.)
height of flagon 9 in. (22.86 cm.). Henley, Suffolk

In the reformed Prayer Books a service at the sick person's house was
introduced, although there was considerable resistance to this service
from both wings of church opinion. On the one hand the Calvinistic
minded churchmen objected because no provision was made for the
preaching of the Word which Calvin insisted was necessary. In 1592
one Robert Southworth was presented to his Archdeacon for refusing
to give the Holy Communion privately to two sick persons at Easter,

PLATE 72. Engraving of The Last Supper on the Paten in the picture above

PLATE 73. Chalice for the sick,
silver gilt; maker's mark *CK*,
1684
height 4¼ in. (10.7 cm.)
St James' Church, Piccadilly,
London

having queried whether it was lawful to celebrate in a private house. In 1633 William Westerley was presented for the same matter. On the other hand, those who might wish to communicate the sick using this service were fearful of being accused of being Papists, using the service as a private Mass. This was a dangerous accusation to face after the outlawing of the Papists in the 1570's, but there were many parishes where it went on quietly and happily. In 1606 the churchwardens' accounts show expenditure of 8d. at Wilmslow, Cheshire, for wine to serve the sick in the parish and women with child; and St Peter Mancroft, Norwich, accounts of 1630 show the expenditure of 6d. for a pint of muskadine (a strong sweet wine made from the muscat grape) for Isaac Girling to receive the Sacrament in times of his sickness; the amount of wine would suggest there must have been several to communicate with him. In 1698 St Michael's, Macclesfield, paid 7s5d. for wine for private communions but it was undoubtedly the care taken of their sick by the Papist priests in the difficult times of James II that brought to the attention of the Anglican faithful this pastoral opportunity for their parish priests.

The vessels used would have been those for the parish communions,

113

PLATE 74. Chalice and Paten for the sick, silver gilt; maker John Keith, London; chalice 1851, paten 1864
height of chalice 4¾ in. (12.06 cm.) diameter of paten 4 in. (10.16 cm.)
From a private collection

but quite obviously their size was inconvenient and so eventually special plate was made for the purpose of communion of the sick.

The first would appear to have been a cup and cover of silver gilt made in 1684 for St James', Piccadilly (Plate 73), where two further cups were added in 1694, the one inscribed "Ye curates priv; communion cup". These special cups are very similar in design to those in general use; some, however, are just bowls on a moulded foot about three inches high without stems, which show a desire to fit the cup for its use with the sick.

Ralph Richardson of Chester made twelve miniature cups between 1721 and 1731, all closely following the design of the larger cups that he made. Many appear to have been the gift of some generous soul and we find them inscribed for the use of the poor, sick communicants in the parish. In 1716, when a complete altar set was given to Charlbury Church, Oxfordshire, it included the usual chalice paten, flagon and alms dish, but added a font, basin and a communion cup for the sick, on the bowl of which is inscribed: "Calix domini: I COR, II v. 27, 1716" and "Infirmus et visitastis me: MAT XXV V. 36".

Then there is at St Peter and St Paul, Dagenham, an Elizabethan, York-made cup of 1598, which was presented in the late seventeenth century and inscribed: "Private communion plate for y parish of Dagenha to be kept by ye minister". There appear to be only about fifty eighteenth-century Communion Cups for the sick left. It would seem that the use of the service, as well as the provision of special vessels, would depend largely upon the churchmanship of the parish; latitudinarians did not care for these things. It was the evangelical movement which gave a new impetus to the Service.

114

Charles Wesley made great use of the service. A clergyman may not publicly officiate in any parish not his own without the permission of the incumbent of the parish which he is visiting, but there is no canon law against any clergyman celebrating the Holy Communion in any sick room anywhere. Thus, Wesley, whose followers were frequently denied a regular sacrament in Church, made the most of celebration with the sick. For example, during the period June 1740 to May 1741 Wesley celebrated 58 weekday sick communions for as many as 19 communicants. His example was followed by the Anglican Evangelicals, and by the early 1800's their diligence in giving communion to the sick was

PLATE 75. Five Communion Sets for the sick
From the collection of the Rev. James Gilchrist

notably an example that was followed in the 1830's and '40's by the Tractarians.

The inconvenience of having no small vessels from the church led to a personal gift to many clergyman of what "The Ecclesiologist" in 1844 called "absurd pocket-cases", one of which, indeed, at St George's, Bloomsbury, was described in the terrier of 1830 as "a toilet set". These consisted of a cup, a paten on a foot and a silver or glass bottle for the wine. The ecclesiologists advised them to be made following the shape of a medieval chalice and paten and the one here illustrated was made by their silversmith, Keith, in 1851. (Plate 74.)

Plate 75 shows a variety of these made between 1840 and 1870. On the top row a set by G. Roberts shows a Grecian influence. In the second row the three vessels on the right are covered with engraving, that on the paten being a representation of Leonardo's *Last Supper*. The set was made in 1849, by Jupp and Woodward of Birmingham. On the left of the central row, the set made in 1861 by A. and S. of Birmingham seems to presage the simplicity of a later age. On the right of the bottom row is a set dated 1840 which is typical of those made by Barnard, and that on the left was made in 1871 by Hands and Son and is the usual version of the High Church Gothic.

These vessels have caught the imagination and affection of many generations of Anglican clergy and have been handed down from parson to parson as they are reminders of many sweet and comforting services. The famous Archdeacon Julius Hare wrote to his brother Augustus Hare, then approaching his death, in February, 1834: "Among other things I have been thinking what memorial I should like to have of you; will you leave me your sacrament cup that which you carry about to the cottages?"

Bibliography

OMAN, Charles *English Church Plate. 597–1830.* 1957.
Authoritative and Definitive.
The Bibliography of County and Diocesan inventories compiled by OMAN is exhaustive. However, since the publication a number of gaps have been filled by the painstaking work of S. A. JEAVONS, F.S.A.
The Church Plate of Derbyshire. 1961.
The Church Plate of Nottinghamshire. 1965.
The Church Plate of Warwickshire, The Diocese of Coventry. 1963.
The Church Plate of the Archdeaconry of Stoke-on-Trent, 1959.
The Church Plate of the Archdeaconry of Salop. 1964.
ARKWRIGHT, D.L. & BOURNE, B.W. *The Church Plate of the Archdeaconry of Ludlow.* 1961.
OMAN, C. *English Medieval Base Metal Church Plate.* 1964.

EXHIBITIONS – CATALOGUES
Silver Plate of Newcastle Manufacture. 1897.
Archaeologia Aeliana. Vol. XXI. 1899.
Church Plate from the Midlands
City Museum & Art Gallery, Birmingham. 1948.
Church Plate from the Diocese of Hereford
Hereford Art Gallery. 1958.
Church Treasures from the Archdeaconry of Suffolk
Blythburgh Church. 1961.
Church Treasures from the Archdeaconry of Ipswich
The Art Gallery, Ipswich. 1965.
Modern Church Plate
City Art Gallery, Manchester.

PERMANENT EXHIBITION
Lincoln Cathedral Treasury
Curator: The Rev. Peter Hawker, Cherry Willingham, Lincoln.

MEDIEVAL INVENTORIES OF CHURCH GOODS
Vetus Liber Archidiaconi Elignensis, c. 1278-c. 1390.
ed. The Rev. C. L. Feltoe, D.D. & E. H. Minns, M.A. 1917.
Archdeaconry of Norwich. Temp. Edward III
Transcribed by Dom. Aelred Watkin. B.P., F.R.Hist. S.Norfolk Record Society. Vol. XIX. Part I & II. 1947–8.
Christchurch Canterbury, 1315 to 18th century
Transcribed & ed. by J. Wickham Legg, F.S.A. & W. H. St John Hope, M.A. 1902.

CHURCH ACCOUNTS
The Medieval Records of a London City Church – St Mary-at-Hill. 1420–1559.
Transcribed & ed. by Henry Littlehales. 1904.
Churchwarden's Accounts of St Edmund & St Thomas. Sarum. 1443–1702.
Henry James Fowle Swayne. 1896.
Cratfield, Accounts of the Parish. 1490–1692.
Transcribed by the Rev. William Holland. B.A.
ed. The Rev. J. J. Raven, D.D., F.S.A. 1895.
Accounts of the Wardens of the Parish of Morebath, Devon. 1520–73.
Transcribed by the Rev. J. Erskine Binney, M.A. 1904.
The County Archaeological and Record Societies publish in their Transactions
numerous inventories and accounts. Also an invaluable general treatment is:
Churchwarden's Accounts from the 14th to close of 17th century
by J. Charles Cox, H.D., F.S.A. 1913.

RELATED WORKS
Addleshaw, G. W. D. & Frederick Etchells, *The Architectural Setting of Anglican
Worship, 1950.*
Alcuin Club Tracts
The Ornaments of the Rubric. by J. T. Micklethwaite, F.S.A.
English or Roman Use, by E. C. P. Wyatt, M.A.
50 Pictures of Gothic Altars by the Rev. Percy Dearmer, M.A.
ANSON, P. F. *Fashions in Church Furnishings.* 1840–1940. 1960.
ANDERSON, M. D. *The Imagery of British Churches.* 1955
COOK, G. H. *Medieval Chantries and Chantry Chapels.* 1947.
COX, J. C. *English Church Fittings Furniture & Accessories,* 1923.
PURCHAS, the Rev. J. *Directorium Anglicanum.* 1858.
SCUDAMORE, the Rev. W. E. *Notitia Eucharistica.* 2nd ed. 1876.
Society of SS Peter & Paul
Pictures of the English Liturgy, Pt. 2. Low Mass. 1916.
TANNER, J.R. *Tudor Constitutional Documents 1485–1603.* 1930.
WHITE, J. F. *The Cambridge Movement.* 1962.

MISCELLANEOUS
THORPE, M. C. *London Church Staves.* 1895.

WORKERS IN CHURCH PLATE 16TH CENTURY
CASLEY, H. C. *An Ipswich Worker of Elizabethan Church Plate Proceedings of
Suffolk Institute of Archaeology Vol. XII. Pt. 2.* 1905.
Suffolk Workers of Elizabethan Church Plate.
Proceedings of Suffolk Institute of Archaeology Vol. XIII. Pt. 1. 1907.
JEAVONS, S. A. *Midland Goldsmiths of the Elizabethan Period*
Transactions of Lichfield & South Staffordshire Archaeological and Historial
Society. Vol. III. 1961–2.

PERIODICALS
Transactions of St. Paul's Ecclesiological Society. 1881.
The Ecclesiologist. 1841–68.
Publications of Warham Guild. 1913.

Index

The figures in **bold type** *refer to illustrations.*